我知道这世上有人在等我，但我不知道他是谁，为了这个，我每天都非常快乐。我无法信口开河，许诺一段没有争执的完美爱情。但是，我保证只要有你的努力经营，我就会不离不弃。

I know someone in the world is waiting for me, although I've no idea of who he is. But I feel happy every day for this. I can't promise you a perfect relationship without arguments. However, I can promise you as long as you're trying, I'm staying.

爱，是最美丽的语言

詹少晶／编译

江苏人民出版社

图书在版编目（CIP）数据

爱，是最美丽的语言：英汉对照 / 詹少晶编译．-- 南京：江苏人民出版社，2016.1
ISBN 978-7-214-17087-3

Ⅰ．①爱… Ⅱ．①詹… Ⅲ．①英语—汉语—对照读物 Ⅳ．① H319.4

中国版本图书馆 CIP 数据核字（2015）第 311104 号

书　　名　爱，是最美丽的语言：英汉对照
编 译 者　詹少晶
责任编辑　朱　超
装帧设计　浪殿设计　飞　扬
版式设计　张文艺
出版发行　凤凰出版传媒股份有限公司
　　　　　江苏人民出版社
出版社地址　南京市湖南路1号A楼，邮编：210009
出版社网址　http://www.jspph.com
　　　　　http://jsrmcbs.tmall.com
经　　销　凤凰出版传媒股份有限公司
印　　刷　北京中印联印务有限公司
开　　本　718 毫米 ×1000 毫米 1/16
印　　张　12
字　　数　153 千字
版　　次　2016 年 5 月第 1 版　2016 年 5 月第 1 次印刷
标准书号　978-7-214-17087-3
定　　价　24.00元

love Is the Most Beautiful Word

爱，是最美丽的语言

爱情是艰难而美好的，它让生活变得更加坚固和温暖；它可以成为生活的食粮，成为白天的太阳，成为黑夜的美梦，成为我们共度的时光中最动听的语言。

目 录 | CONTENTS

两个人的浪漫

爱因艰难而珍贵

爱是最美的语言

曾有一个人，爱我如生命

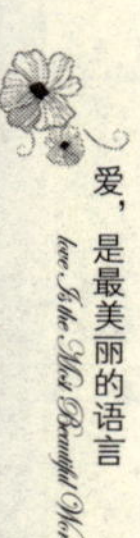

两个人的浪漫

Once I thought love meant flowers, gifts and sweet kisses. But from this experience, I understand that love is just a thread in the quilt of our life. Love is inside, making life strong and warm.

鲜花、礼物和甜蜜的亲吻。可这件事让我明白，爱就像是隐藏在生活这床被子里的线。爱是内在的，它让生活变得更加坚固和温暖。

Love Is Just a Thread
爱只是一根线

◎ Cathyma

Sometimes I really doubt whether there is love between my parents. Every day they are very busy trying to earn money in order to pay the high tuition for my brother and me. They don't act in the romantic ways that I read in books or I see on TV. In their opinion, "I love you" is too **luxurious**[①] for them to say. Sending flowers to each other on Valentine's Day is even more out of the question. Finally my father has a bad temper. When he's very tired from the hard work, it is easy for him to lose his temper.

One day, my mother was sewing a **quilt**[②]. I silently sat down beside her and looked at her.

"Mom, I have a question to ask you," I said after a while.

"What?" she replied, still doing her work.

"Is there love between you and Dad?" I asked her in a very low voice.

My mother stopped her work and raised her head with surprise in her eyes. She didn't answer immediately. Then she bowed her head and continued to sew the quilt.

I was very worried because I thought I had hurt her. I was in a great

① luxurious [lʌg'ʒu:riəs] adj. 奢华的，舒适的
② quilt [kwilt] n. 被子，被褥

美丽语录

Happiness is to look for a warm person for a lifetime.

幸福，就是找一个温暖的人过一辈子。

有时候，我真怀疑父母之间是否还有爱。他们每天都忙着给我和弟弟挣那高昂的学费。他们从未像我在书中读到，或者在电视上看到的那样互诉衷肠。在他们看来，“我爱你”太奢侈了，他们说不出口。在情人节给彼此送上一束花那就更不可能了。我父亲脾气不好。他常常会在劳累了一天之后乱发脾气。

一天，母亲正在缝被子。我静静地坐在她旁边看着她。

“妈，我有个问题想问你。”过了一会儿我说道。

“什么？”她一边继续缝着，一边答道。

“您跟爸爸之间还有没有爱情啊？”我低声问她。

母亲停下手中的活，满眼诧异地抬起头。她没有立刻回答，而是低下头，继续缝被子。

我担心我伤害了她。我尴尬极了，不知道该如何是好。不过，随后我

embarrassment and I didn't know what I should do. But at last I heard my mother say the following words:

"Susan," she said thoughtfully, "Look at this thread. Sometimes it appears, but most of it disappears in the quilt. The thread really makes the quilt strong and durable. If life is a quilt, then love should be a thread. It can hardly be seen anywhere or anytime, but it's really there. Love is inside."

I listened carefully but I couldn't understand her until the next spring. At that time, my father suddenly got sick seriously. My mother had to stay with him in the hospital for a month. When they returned from the hospital, they both looked very pale. It seemed both of them had had a serious illness.

After they were back, every day in the morning and dusk, my mother helped my father walk slowly on the country road. My father had never been so gentle. It seemed they were the most harmonious couple. Along the country road, there were many beautiful flowers, green grass and trees. The sun gently glistened① through the leaves. All of these made up the most beautiful picture in the world.

The doctor had said my father would recover in two months. But after two months he still couldn't walk by himself. All of us were worried about him.

"Dad, how are you feeling now?" I asked him one day.

"Susan, don't worry about me." he said gently. "To tell you the truth, I just like walking with your mom. I like this kind of life." Reading his eyes, I know he loves my mother deeply.

Once I thought love meant flowers, gifts and sweet kisses. But from this experience, I understand that love is just a thread in the quilt of our life. Love is inside, making life strong and warm...

---

① glisten ['glisn] v. 闪耀，发光

听见母亲说：

“苏珊，”她若有所思地说道，“看看这些线。有的时候，你能看得见它们，但大多数时候它们都隐藏在被子里。这些线的确让被子变得更加耐用。如果生活是床被子的话，那么爱就是其中的线。你不可能随时随地看到它，但它却是真实存在的。爱是内在的。”

我听得很仔细，但直到来年春天，我才真正理解她的这番话。那时，我的父亲突然得了重病。母亲需要在医院里照顾他一个月。当他们从医院回家时，两个人看上去都十分苍白，好像他们俩都得了重病一样。

他们回来之后，每个清晨和黄昏，母亲都要搀扶着父亲在乡间小路上散步。我的父亲从未如此温柔过。他们就像是天作之合。小路两旁点缀着许多美丽的鲜花、绿草和树木。阳光透过树叶的缝隙，温柔地洒在地面上。这一切组成了一幅世间最美好的画。

医生说父亲将在两个月内康复。可两个月后，他仍然无法独立行走，我们都很替他担心。

“爸爸，你现在感觉怎么样？”一天，我问他道。

“苏珊，别为我担心。”他温和地说道，“实话告诉你吧，我只是喜欢和你妈妈一起散步的感觉。我喜欢这种生活。”从他的眼神里，我读到他对母亲深深的爱。

曾经我认为爱情就是鲜花、礼物和甜蜜的亲吻。可这件事让我明白，爱就像是隐藏在生活这床被子里的线。爱是内在的，它让生活变得更加坚固和温暖……

Just Two for Breakfast
两个人的早餐

◎ Joe

When my husband and I celebrated our 38th wedding **anniversary**① at our favorite restaurant, Lenny, the piano player, asked, “How did you do it?”

I knew there was no simple answer, but as the weekend approached, I wondered if one reason might be our ritual of breakfast in bed every Saturday and Sunday.

It all started with the breakfast tray my mother gave us as a wedding gift. It had a glass top and slatted wooden side pockets for the morning paper the kind you used to see in the movies. Mother loved her movies, and although she rarely had breakfast in bed, she held high hopes for her daughter. My **adoring**② bridegroom took the message to heart.

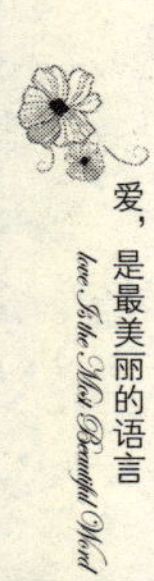

Feeling guilty, I suggested we take turns. Despite grumblings—“hate crumbs in my bed”—Sunday morning found my spouse eagerly awaiting his tray. Soon these weekend breakfasts became such a part of our lives that I never even

① anniversary [ˌæni'vəːsəri] n. 周年纪念日；结婚周年日

② adoring ['ədɔːriŋ] adj. 崇拜的；爱慕的

美丽语录

Love is when you take away the feelings, the passion, the romance, you find out you still care for that person.

所谓爱，就是当感觉、热情和浪漫统统拿掉之后，你仍然珍惜对方。

当我和丈夫在我们最喜欢的饭馆庆祝结婚 38 周年纪念日时，那个钢琴手莱尼过来问道：“你们是怎么过来的？”

我知道，这个问题无法简简单单地来回答。但随着周末的临近，我开始在想：或许其中的一个原因就是我们每个星期六和星期天都在床上吃早餐。

这一切都是从那个早餐托盘开始的，它是妈妈送给我们的结婚礼物。它有一个玻璃盘面，两边各有一个放早报用的细长的木制侧袋，就像过去在电影中见到的那样。我妈很喜欢那些电影，虽然她自己很少在床上用早餐，却非常希望她的女儿能这样。深爱着我的新郎把我母亲的话牢记在心。

出于心里的愧疚感，我提议我们两个轮流准备早餐。星期天早上，虽然他嘴上嘟嘟囔囔地抱怨着——“我讨厌面包屑弄到床上”——但我还是见到丈夫在急切地等候他的早餐。不久，周末早餐就成为我们生活的一部

thought about them. I only knew we treasured this separate, blissful time read, relax, forget the things we should remember.

Sifting through the years, I recalled how our weekends changed, but that we still preserved the ritual. We started our family (as new parents, we slept after breakfast more than we read), but we always found our way back to where we started, just two for breakfast, one on Saturday and one on Sunday.

When we had more time, my tray became more festive. First it was fruit slices placed in **geometric**① pattern; then came flowers from our garden, sometimes just one blossom sprouting from a grapefruit half. This arranger of mine had developed a flair for decorating, using everything from amaryllis to the buds of a maple tree. My husband said my cooking inspired him. Mother would have approved. Perhaps it was the Saturday when the big strawberry wore a daisy hat that I began to think, how can I top this? One dark winter night I woke with a vision of a snowman on a tray. That Sunday I scooped a handful of snow and in no time had my man made. With a flourish I put a miniature pinecone on his head.

As I delivered the tray, complete with a nicely frozen snowman, I waited for a reaction. There was none but as I headed down the stairs I heard a whoop of laughter and then, "You've won! Yes, sir, you've won the prize!"

① geometric [dʒiə'metrik] adj. 几何图案的；成几何级数增加的

分，习以为常也就不去想它了。我只知道我俩都很珍视这段与其他时间有别的幸福时光——看看报，放松放松，忘记那些本该记在心里的事情。

细想逝去的岁月，我回忆起我们周末生活的诸多变化，但这个老习惯依然保留了下来。我们建立起我们的家庭（初为父母时，早饭后我们更多是睡一会儿，而不是阅读），但是我们总能够找到归路，返回原点——只是两个人的早餐，星期六一次，星期天一次。

当我们有了更多的时间，我的早餐托盘上就变得更加具有喜庆色彩。开始时是以几何图形排列的水果片，随后是从自家花园里摘来的鲜花——有时候只是一朵，开在一半的葡萄柚当中。没想到这竟激发出我在装饰、点缀方面的天赋，各种各样的东西，从孤挺花到枫树的叶芽，都成为我手下的装饰材料。丈夫说我做的早餐启发了他，妈妈也会赞同他的说法。或许是在那个星期六，在一个大草莓上放一个雏菊做帽子之后，我开始想，我怎么才能够超过它？在一个漆黑的冬夜，我从梦中醒来，仿佛看到眼前有一个雪人站在托盘上。就在那个星期天，我铲来了一捧雪，很快就做好了一个雪人。我轻轻地把一个微型松果按在雪人的头上。

我端着早餐上楼，盘面上放着那个冻结实的小雪人，我期待着他的反应——什么也没有——但就在我下楼时，我听到他的大笑声："你赢了！毫无疑问，你得奖了！"

Men's Romantic

男人的浪漫

◎ Dr. Nancy kalish

We too often define "romantic" in women's terms— sending flowers and cards, saving **mementos**① and putting them in a box or scrapbook, gushing over chick romance movies, or listening to romantic songs all day.

Men may not do these things, but many men do something more romantic than all that: they keep their love in their hearts forever.

My survey of 3000 men and women worldwide who tried **reunions**② with lost loves asked, "How long did it take for you to get over your lost love?" Responses from the men indicated that they took significantly longer to get over their lost loves than the women. Some of the men were not satisfied with the survey choices: the last choice listed was, "Over 10 years." Only men crossed out all the choices and wrote, "I never got over her!" While no doubt some women never got over their lost loves, either, only men wrote this comment on the survey.

Adolescent boys are "not supposed" to cry over lost loves. But many of my

① memento [mi'mentəu] n. 纪念物；引起回忆的东西

② reunion [riː'juːnjən] n. 再会合；团聚，重聚

美丽语录

In this world, only those men who really feel happy can give women happiness.

在这个世界上，只有真正快乐的男人，才能带给女人真正的快乐。

我们常常太过于将“浪漫”定义为女人的专属名词——送鲜花和贺卡，在盒子或剪贴簿中收藏纪念品，滔滔不绝地谈论少女类的爱情电影，或者整天听情歌。

男人大概不会做这些事，但很多男人会做比这更浪漫的事：他们将爱永存在心中。

我在调查里问那些想重归于好的3000名男士和女士：“你要花多长时间从失恋中走出来？”男人们的回答表明他们比女人要花更长的时间才能恢复。有些男人不满意调查的选项，最后一个选项为“超过十年”。只有男人划了所有的选项，并写道“我绝不会忘记她！”毫无疑问，有些女士也会对失去的爱无法忘怀，然而只有男士在调查中写了这项意见。

青春期男生“不应该”在失恋后哭泣。但是我的很多男性受访者表示，

male participants reported that, after their high school girlfriends broke up with them, they cried in private, every night, for months.

My lost love reunion findings about romantic men paralleled results of my survey of adults who never tried lost love reunions. There were significantly more men than women who chose to fill out the survey, and they expressed strong feelings for their first loves, even though they had not contacted these women (and may never do so).

Posts on the Message Board of my web site (Lostlovers.com), are more represented by women than men. But appearances are **misleading**[①]. Actually, there are more men who are members of my site than women. The men don't post as often as the women, but they are reading!

Men more often sign up for private phone consultations to talk about their lost loves than women.

But it is a rare men's magazine that will print a story about love and romance. The editors tell me that they think men are uninterested. Not so! When my research was quoted in Playboy, it generated a lot of responses.

On occasions where romance is expected (such as Valentine's Day, birthdays or anniversaries), we should all remember to separate emotions from behaviors. Men may not make scrapbooks of mementos of their love experiences, but they are every bit as loving, loyal, and yes, romantic, as women—and sometimes more so!

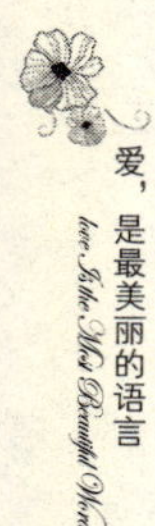

① misleading [mis'li:diŋ] adj. 使人误解的；骗人的，迷惑人的

他们高中时期与女友分手后，好几个月里每天夜晚都会独自流泪。

在调查报告中，那些想重归于好的人和那些不再试图找回失去的爱恋的人相比，均衡结果显示更多男士比女士选择来填这项调查，并且他们表达了对初恋的强烈感情，即使他们已经和这些女人没有任何接触了（而且可能永远都不会这么做）。

我的网站（Lostlovers.com）留言板上的留言更多是女士发表的言论，但这只是表面现象。实际上，在我的网站上男士会员要多过女士。男人们不会像女士那样经常回应，但是他们会去阅读留言。

与女士相比，男士更愿意参加私下的电话咨询谈论他们失去的爱情。

但是，男性杂志很少会刊登关于爱情或浪漫的故事。编辑告诉我，他们认为男士对这些不感兴趣。绝不是！当我的研究被《花花公子》引用时，它得到了大量的回应。

有时浪漫是令人期待的（比如情人节、生日或纪念日），我们应该记住把情感和行动区分开来。男人也许不会做纪念品剪贴簿等留下爱情历程中令人回忆的东西，但是他们和女人们一样爱着，一样忠诚。是的，他们同女人一样浪漫——有时，甚至比女人更浪漫！

Why We Love Who We Love

打破砂锅爱到底

◎ Joyce Brothers

Have you ever known a married couple that just didn't seem as though they should fit together—yet they are both happy in the marriage, and you can't figure out why?

I know of one couple: He is a **burly**[①] ex-athlete who, in addition to being a successful salesman, coaches Little League, is active in his Rotary Club and plays golf every Saturday with friends. Meanwhile, his wife is petite, quiet and a complete Homebody. She doesn't even like to go out to dinner.

What mysterious force drives us into the arms of one person, while pushing us away from another who might appear equally desirable to any **unbiased**[②] observer?

Of the many factors influencing our idea of the perfect mate, one of the most telling, according to John Money, professor emeritus of medical psychology and pediatrics at Johns Hopkins University, is what he calls our "love map"—a group of messages encoded in our brains that describes our likes and dislikes.

---

① burly ['bə:li] adj. 魁梧的，强壮的；粗鲁的；率直的

② unbiased ['ʌn'baiəst] adj. 无偏见的，不偏不倚的，公正的

美丽语录

Just be yourself and one day you will find someone who loves you for everything you are.

做最真实的自己就好了，总有一天你会找到一个人，他（她）会爱上你的一切。

你是否听说过这样一对夫妻，他们看起来并不般配——却婚姻幸福，家庭美满，令人百思不得其解?

我就知道这样一对夫妻：他是一名身材魁梧的退役运动员，还是一个成功的销售员，另外还在一家俱乐部当教练；除此之外，他还热心于扶轮社的各项事务，每周六都要和朋友打高尔夫球。然而，他的妻子天生娇小柔弱，喜欢安静，完全一副以家庭为中心的样子。甚至最好连外出吃饭都别叫上她。

那么，当我们遇上在外人看来同样出色的两个人时，是什么样的神秘力量让我们对一个人投怀送抱，而对另一个人敬而远之呢?

约翰·霍普金斯大学临床医学小儿科的荣誉退休教授约翰·莫尼认为，在影响我们择偶的众多因素中，最重要的因素之一就是他所谓的“爱的蓝图”——一组在大脑中描述我们喜好的编码信息，它显示了我们多方面的

It shows our preferences in hair and eye color, in voice, smell, and body build. It also records the kind of personality that appeals to us, whether it's the warm and friendly type or the strong, silent type.

In short, we fall for and pursue those people who most clearly fit our love map. And this love map is largely determined in childhood. By age eight, the pattern for our ideal mate has already begun to float around in our brains.

When I lecture, I often ask couples in the audience what drew them to their dates or mates. Answers range from "She's strong and independent" and "I go for redheads" to "I love his sense of humor" and "That crooked smile, that's what did it."

Robert Winch, a longtime sociology professor at Northwestern University, stated in his research that our choice of a marriage partner involves a number of social similarities. But he also maintained that we look for someone with complementary needs. A talker is attracted to someone who likes to listen, or an aggressive personality may seek out a more passive partner.

However, there are instances where people of different social backgrounds end up getting married and being extremely happy. I know of one man, a factory worker from a traditional Irish family in Chicago, who fell in love with an African American Baptist. When they got married, their friends and relatives predicted a quick failure. But 25 years later, the marriage is still strong.

It turns out that the woman was like her mother-in-law—a loving and caring person, the type who rolls up her sleeves and volunteers to work at church or help out people in need. This is the quality that her husband fell for, and it made color and religion and any other social factors irrelevant to him.

Or as George Burns, who was Jewish and married the Irish Catholic Gracie

偏好，如头发、眼球颜色、声音、气味、体格等等，同时它也记录了对我们有吸引力的性格特征——是热情友好，还是刚强内敛。

简而言之，我们常常会倾心于并强烈追求那些与我们的“爱的蓝图”相吻合的人。我们的“爱的蓝图”早在童年时期就基本成型了。8 岁时，我们的脑中就会开始浮现理想伴侣的形象。

开讲座时，我常常问台下的夫妻听众们，到底是什么让他们开始约会，并最终走到一起的。我得到的答案五花八门、千奇百怪，从“她很坚强、独立”说到“我喜欢红头发的人”，从“我喜欢他的幽默感”聊到“就是他那坏坏的微笑。”

西北大学资深的社会学教授罗伯特·威奇曾经在他的研究报告中说道，我们对婚姻伴侣的选择涵盖了一系列社会共性。然而，他也坚持，我们在寻找伴侣时也是为了满足互补的需求。善于聆听的人钟情于能说会道的人，个性好强的人则会寻找性格温婉的人。

然而，也不乏一些社会背景相差悬殊，却能喜结连理、幸福美满的人。我就认识这样一个男人。他是一名工厂工人，来自芝加哥一个传统的爱尔兰家庭。他爱上了一位非裔美国浸礼会教徒。当他们结婚时，亲朋好友都觉得他们的婚姻不会长久。但是，如今 25 年过去了，他们的婚姻依旧那样牢不可破。

原来那个女人像她的婆婆一样，善解人意、温婉可人、富有同情心。她甘愿挽起衣袖在教堂里干活，或者为那些有需要的人们伸出援手。这就是她的丈夫觉得她的可爱之处。肤色、宗教以及其他一些社会因素之类的东西，在他眼中都不算什么。

Allen, used to say: his marriage was his favorite gig, even though it was Gracie who got all the laughs. The two of them did share certain social similarities—both grew up in the city, in large but poor families. Yet what really drew them together was evident from the first time they went onstage together. They complemented each other perfectly: he was the straight man, and she delivered the punch lines.

There are certainly such "odd couples" who could scarcely be happier. We all know some drop-dead beautiful person married to an unusually plain wallflower. This is a trade-off some call the equity theory.

When men and women possess a particular asset, such as high intelligence, unusual beauty, a personality that makes others swoon, or a hefty bankroll that has the same effect, some decide to trade their assets for someone else's strong points. The raging beauty may trade her luster for the power and security that come with big bucks. The not-so-talented fellow from a good family may swap his pedigree for a poor but brilliantly talented mate.

Indeed, almost any combination can survive and thrive. Once, some neighbors of mine stopped by for a friendly social engagement. During the evening, Robert, a man in his 50s, suddenly blurted out, "What would you say if your daughter planned to marry someone who has a ponytail and insisted on doing the cooking?"

"Unless your daughter loves cooking," I responded, "I'd say she was darn lucky."

"Exactly," his wife agreed. "It's really your problem, Robert—that old macho thing rearing its head again. The point is, they're in love."

I tried to reassure Robert, pointing out that the young man their daughter

又比如说乔治·伯恩斯，他是犹太人，却和天主教徒格雷西·艾伦结婚。过去他常说，就算格雷西骑在自己头上，婚姻也是他最宝贵的财富。他们俩的确有一些共同的社会经历：他们都在大城市长大，都来自穷苦的大家庭。然而，真正让他们走到一起的是他们第一次一起登上舞台的经历。他们的性格互补得恰到好处：乔治性格直率，格雷西则妙语连珠。

当然，也有一些例外，这类"不般配的夫妻"生活得并不幸福。我们都知道，有些光彩照人的"白天鹅"和平平无奇的"丑小鸭"步入婚姻殿堂，这也许就是人们所说的等价平衡理论吧！

当男人和女人们拥有某种过人之处时，比如聪明绝顶，相貌出众，个性独具魅力，财力雄厚，那么他们中有些人就会用自己的优点来换取别人的长处。出众的美貌可能成为她换取权势、金钱和安全感的资本。家底殷实却并不出众的小伙子则可以用他的富贵出身虏获一位贫寒而聪慧的女孩的芳心。

诚然，几乎任何一种结合都存在幸福的可能。一次，邻居们过来串门。晚上的时候，五十多岁的罗伯特突然脱口而出："如果你们的女儿嫁给一个绑着马尾，并执意要下厨房的人，你们会怎么样？"

"除非你的女儿酷爱美食，"我答道，"否则我会说她走了狗屎运了。"

"没错，"他的妻子同意我的说法，"那就是你的问题咯，罗伯特！——你的大男子主义又来了，关键是他们彼此相爱。"

我试着让罗伯特放宽心，对他说，他女儿选择的那个年轻小伙子为人

had picked out seemed to be a relaxed, nonjudgmental sort of person—a trait he shared with her own mother.

Is there such a thing as love at first sight? Why not? When people become love-struck, what happens in that instant is the couple probably discover a unique something they have in common. It could be something as **mundane**① as they both were reading the same book or were born in the same town. At the same time they recognize some trait in the other that complements their own personality.

I happen to be one of those who were struck by the magic wand. On that fateful weekend, while I was a sophomore at Cornell University, I had a terrible cold and hesitated to join my family on vacation in the Catskill Mountains. Finally I decided anything would be better than sitting alone in my dormitory room.

That night as I was preparing to go to dinner, my sister rushed up the stairs and said, "When you walk into that dining room, you're going to meet the man you'll marry."

I think I said something like "Buzz off!" But my sister couldn't have been more right. I knew it from the moment I saw him, and the memory still gives me goose flesh. He was a premed student, also at Cornell, who incidentally also had a bad cold. I fell in love with Milton the instant I met him.

Milt and I were married for 39 years, until his death in 1989. And all that time we experienced a love that Erich Fromm called a "feeling of fusion, of oneness," even while we both continued to change, grow and fulfill our lives.

① mundane ['mʌndein] adj. 世俗的；世界的；平凡的

随和，不专制，就像她妈妈一样。

真的有一见钟情这回事吗？为什么没有呢？当爱情来临的时候，那一刻无论如何，爱侣们总能找到他们惺惺相惜的地方。这些地方可能很平常：比如他们曾经读过同一本书，或者他们出生在同一个小镇。与此同时，他们还会看到双方性格的互补之处。

巧的是，我也曾经被爱情魔棒击中。在那个命中注定的周末，那时我还是康奈尔大学二年级的学生，当时得了重感冒，正犹豫着要不要随家人一起到卡茨基尔山度假。最后，我还是决定去了，因为无论怎样总比一个人待在宿舍里强。

那天晚上，我正要去赴宴的时候，妹妹冲上楼对我说："当你走进那家餐厅的时候，你就会看到你的白马王子。"

我想我当时说了句"走开"之类的话。可是，果然被她说中了。当我见到他的那一刻，我就知道是他了。这样的记忆至今回想起来仍会让我浑身起鸡皮疙瘩。他是医科大的预科生，也在康奈尔大学，更巧的是，他也得了重感冒。从我第一眼看到米尔顿，我就爱上了他。

到 1989 年米尔特去世，我们结婚 39 年了。一直以来，我们共同经历着艾瑞克·弗洛姆所说的那份融合之情，合二为一的爱恋。甚至当我们不断蜕变，共同成长，仍旧一起履行着我们的生命之约。

A Small Harbor of Reconnection

让爱重温的小港

© Karen Scalf Linamen

It was December in California, and we had flown in from Texas to visit our families for the holidays. The days between our arrival and Christmas Eve brimmed with a **flurry**[①] of last minute activities.

One evening we all hustled into the car to drive to a Christmas party at the home of family friends. We were a little behind schedule because my mom, sister, and I had gotten home late after spending a long day writing checks, signing charge slips, and bringing **hysterical**[②] grins of joy to the faces of local merchants at a nearby mall.

My mom looked across the front seat at my dad and said, "Whew! What a busy day! I feel like I haven't seen you in a week!"

My dad grunted, checked the rearview mirror, and changed lanes at something **approximating**[③] the speed of light.

My mom reached over and twirled a lock of my dad's hair around her finger. "I know! Let's look at each other. For just a minute. In the eyes."

---

① flurry ['flʌri] n. 阵风，小阵雪；慌张，混乱

② hysterical [his'terikəl] adj. 歇斯底里的；情绪异常激动的

③ approximate [ə'prɔksimit] adj. 近似的，接近的；大约的

美丽语录

Love me little and love me long.

不求情意绵绵，但求天长地久。

加利福利亚的 12 月，我们从德克萨斯州乘飞机来到这里和家人一起过圣诞节。从我们到达的那天起，直到平安夜，时间都被名目繁多的岁末活动挤得满满当当。

一天晚上，我们挤上一辆车，去亲戚朋友家参加圣诞晚会。因为妈妈、姐姐和我在附近的商场疯狂购物了一整天，不停地填支票、签交费单，让附近购物中的商人们笑开花了，直到很晚才回家，所以我们出发的时间已经比原计划晚了些。

妈妈看着在前排开车的爸爸说："哎呀，今天真是繁忙的一天啊！我感觉有一个星期没见到你了！"

爸爸嘴里咕哝了几句，一边看后视镜，一边转换车道，车速已经接近光速了。

妈妈伸出手缠绕着爸爸的一捋头发，说道："我知道了！我们互相注视着对方吧，就一会儿，看着对方的眼睛。"

My dad responded this time. He groaned. "Honey, I'm driving."

"Ten seconds. Five! I haven't seen you all day. I need to look into your eyes. Are you ready?"

He shook his head. "I can't look right now. We'll have a wreck!"

"At the next light."

At the speed we were traveling, we hit the next red light in no time. And sure enough, holding hands across the front seat, my parents turned and gazed into each other's eyes. "Hi," my mom said. "Hi," my dad said warmly back.

Then the light changed, the gas pedal hit the floor, and the race was on again. Nothing had changed, and yet everything had changed. Most of all, I was silently moved by what I had witnessed: a small harbor of reconnection in a raging hurricane of activity and distraction.

爸爸这次说话了，他咕哝道："亲爱的，我在开车呢！"

"就看 10 秒钟。5 秒！我已经一整天没看见你了。我需要注视你的眼睛。准备好了吗？"

爸爸摇了摇头："我现在不能看你。否则我们会撞车的。"

"那就等下一个红灯的时候！"

我们的车子飞快地行驶着，不一会就赶上了红灯。果然，父亲转过身，隔着前座和母亲手握着手，深情地注视着对方的眼睛。"嗨！"妈妈说。"嗨！"爸爸热情地回应道。

这时，绿灯亮了，油门踩到底，赛车又开始了。好像一切都没有改变，又好像一切都变了。最重要的是，刚刚亲眼看到的那一幕已经悄悄地打动了我：在这手忙脚乱、焦头烂额的日子里，居然还有这样让爱重温的小港湾。

Roller Romance

滚轴浪漫曲

© Stephenie Ray Brown

In the spring of 1980, I had been following one particular guy around school for a month. I just did not have the nerve to go up and talk to him. An embarrassing situation, from that winter, truly prevented me from approaching him.

He had been a starter for the junior varsity basketball team and I was a cheerleader, I had many opportunities to see this gorgeous guy in action. That is, if I wore my glasses. You see, I am as blind as a bat and was too **vain**① to wear them.

As Terry sank a half court shot at the last second, this extremely near-sighted cheerleader, misidentified the hero and began cheering for the wrong guy. As the crowd started chuckling, my face turned crimson as Terry walked by me to get to the locker room. Months later, he only knew me as the dingy cheerleader who could not even get his name right when he hit a great shot!

However, my best friend attended church with Terry. Shirley decided to play matchmaker. She not only invited me to a church-sponsored skating

① vain [vein] adj. 爱虚荣的，自负的；徒然的，无益的

美丽语录

Destiny determines who comes into our lives but it's the heart that decides who stays inside.

命运决定谁会进入我们的生活，内心决定我们与谁并肩。

1980 年的春天，我已经在学校内外追随那个男孩整整一个月了。我只是没有勇气走上前和他说话。自从那个冬天发生了一件令人尴尬的事情之后，我就更加没有勇气接近他了。

当时，他是学校篮球二对三年级的队员，而我是啦啦队队长，所以我有很多机会欣赏这个球艺精湛的男孩的表演。只是，我需要戴上眼睛。你也知道，我视力不好，就像蝙蝠那样瞎，但是虚荣心却使我不想戴眼镜。

半决赛中，特里在最后一秒投篮命中，我这个视力差到极点的啦啦队队长却把英雄认错了，一个劲地为另一个人喝彩。在场的观众开始轻声讥笑，我的脸涨得通红。特里从我身边走过，进了更衣室。于是，接下来的几个月，他对我的印象都只是那个在他投中好球时，却把他的名字弄错的糟糕的啦啦队队长。

然而，我最好的朋友常常和特里一起去教堂做礼拜。雪莉决定充当我们俩的媒人。她不仅邀请我参加一个教堂组织的溜冰派对，还把我推进特

party, but also literally pushed me in his parents' car to ride to the skating rink. Although the skating rink was 15 miles away, very few words were spoken. As I sank down in that backseat, I just wanted to keep sinking. This had truly been a huge mistake.

After we arrived at the skating rink, things did not get any better. Each couple skate I hoped and prayed that Terry would ask me. He didn't! After about three couple skates, I decided enough was enough! So I took turns skating with his two best friends. As the last call for a couple skate came over the rink's loud speakers, Terry finally skated somewhat awkwardly and stood beside the rails with me.

"I guess you wonder why I have not asked you to couple skate?" were his first words to me. Trying ever so hard not to look in those big beautiful brown eyes that made me melt, I answered **nonchalantly**① and dishonestly, "No, not really."

This guy not only ignored my tart reply, but would also win my heart with the following reply. Casting those beautiful eyes down at his skates, he humbly remarked, "I didn't ask because I do not skate very well. If you are not afraid that I will make you fall, would you please skate with me?" This time I did look into those eyes and did melt.

As we skated hand in hand to Always and Forever, I knew my life would never be the same. I never knew a guy that actually would admit any of his faults, let alone worry about a girl to boot! I had first been attracted to his beauty on the outside (who wouldn't notice those beautiful brown eyes), but it would be his beautiful heart that made me realize how truly special he was.

---

① nonchalantly ['nɔnʃələntli] adv. 漠不关心地；冷淡地

里父母的车，接着车就这样向溜冰场开去。虽然溜冰场离这儿有 15 英里远，可我们谁也没有说话。我坐在车后排，一心想着钻进座位里去。这真是一个巨大的错误。

我们到达溜冰场后，情况并没有好转。每当有双人滑的时候，我都企盼特里能过来邀请我。可他却没有那样做！大约三场双人滑结束后，我实在忍无可忍了！于是我和他最好的两个朋友轮流滑着。当溜冰场的喇叭里想起最后一场双人滑即将开始时，特里终于笨拙地溜到栏杆旁，和我站在了一起。

“我猜你肯定很奇怪我为什么不邀请你和我一起双人滑。”这是他第一次对我说话。我试着不去看他那双可以将我融化的美丽的棕色眼睛。我假装镇定，还对他撒了谎：“不，我并没有那么想。”

这个家伙不但不把我刻薄的回答放在心上，还用下面这些回答俘虏了我的心。他那漂亮的双眼盯着自己的溜冰鞋，谦虚地说道：“我之所以没有邀请你，是因为我滑得不好。如果你不怕我会让你摔倒的话，你愿意和我一起滑吗？”这一次，我看了那双眼睛，我真的被他融化了。

就在我们手牵手向着“永远”滑去的时候，我知道我的生活将从此刻开始改变。我从来没见过一个会承认自己缺点的男孩，更别说还会为一个女孩担心。刚开始我只是被他英俊的外表吸引（有谁能不注意到那双美丽的棕色眼睛呢），但是，他那颗美丽的心灵让我真正明白他有多特别。

I had actually found my Prince Charming.

Even though he was not riding on a handsome steed (but rented roller skates), he made me feel like Cinderella at the ball as we skated around the rink. I clung tightly to his hand—not because I was afraid of midnight—but to help keep him from falling. When I look at our wedding pictures, my favorite is walking down the aisle as husband and wife. Most couples walk down the aisle with the bride's hand tucked **neatly**① in the crook of her husband's arm. Not us! We walked down the aisle, after being pronounced man and wife, just like we had done seven years before at that skating rink—hand-in-hand with the promise of helping keep the other one from falling.

Our children love to hear the story of how their dad did not know how to skate and asked me to hold his hand to help us keep from tumbling. But it had already been too late for their mother. Only after one look into those eyes, she had fallen—fallen in love with Prince Charming.

① neatly ['ni:tli] adv. 整洁地；灵巧地，利索地；恰好地越的

我终于找到我的白马王子了。

即使他并没有骑着骏马（只是穿着租来的溜冰鞋），然而当我们绕着溜冰场滑行时，他给我的感觉就仿佛我是舞会上的灰姑娘。我紧紧地拉住他的手——并不是因为我害怕午夜——而是为了帮助他，不让他摔倒。当我看着我们的结婚照时，我最喜欢的一张是夫妻二人沿着教堂过道向外走去。大多数夫妻从过道走过时，都是妻子把手优雅地放在丈夫的臂弯里。我们可不是这样的！在宣布成为夫妻后，我们走过道时就像是 7 年前我们在溜冰场上那样——手牵着手，许下诺言不让对方摔倒。

我们的孩子最喜欢听的故事，就是他们的爸爸不知道怎么滑冰，让我牵着他的手防止摔倒的事。可是那时候，对他们的妈妈来说已经为时已晚，因为她只是看了那双眼睛一眼，就已经深陷其中，深深地爱上了她的白马王子。

Words from the Hearts

说出心里话

◎ Ellen Frankenstein

Most people need to hear those "three little words" I love you. Once in a while, they hear them just in time.

I met Connie the day she was admitted to the **hospice**① ward, where I worked as a volunteer. Her husband, Bill, stood nervously nearby as she was transferred from the gurney to the hospital bed. Although Connie was in the final stages of her fight against cancer, she was alert and cheerful. We got her settled in. I finished marking her name on all the hospital supplies she would be using, and then asked if she needed anything.

"Oh, yes," she said, "would you please show me how to use the TV? I enjoy the soaps so much and I don't want to get behind on what's happening." Connie was a romantic. She loved soap operas, romance novels and movies with a good love story. As we became acquainted, she confided how frustrating it was to be married 32 years to a man who often called her "a silly woman."

"Oh, I know Bill loves me," she said, "but he has never been one to say he loves me, or send cards to me." She sighed and looked out the window at the

① hospice ['hɔspis] n. 旅客住宿处；收容所

美丽语录

I will grow old, so will you. But those love words I say to you will never get old.

我会老，你会老，可是那些我说给你的情话不会老。

大多数人需要听到那“三个小字”——我爱你。每隔一段时间，他们就会在最需要的时候听到。

我在康尼住进收容所病房的那天见到她。我在那儿当志愿者。把她从轮床抬上病床时，她的丈夫比尔紧张地站在旁边。虽然康尼处于和癌症搏斗的晚期，但她仍然神智清醒，精神愉快。我们把她安顿好。我在她要使用的所有住院用品上标上她的名字，然后问她是否需要什么。

“啊，是的，”她说，“请告诉我怎么用电视，好吗？我非常喜欢连续剧，想随时跟进剧情进展。”康尼是个浪漫的人。她酷爱肥皂剧、言情小说和描述美好爱情故事的电影。随着我们越来越熟，她向我吐露道，跟一个经常叫她“傻女人”的男人生活了 32 年有多么沮丧。

“唉，我知道比尔爱我，”她说道，“可是他从来不说他爱我，或者寄贺卡给我。”她叹了口气，朝窗外庭院里的树望去。“如果他说声‘我爱你’，

trees in the courtyard. "I'd give anything if he'd say 'I love you,' but it's just not in his nature."

Bill visited Connie every day. In the beginning, he sat next to the bed while she watched the soaps. Later, when she began sleeping more, he paced up and down the hallway outside her room. Soon, when she no longer watched television and had fewer waking moments, I began spending more of my volunteer time with Bill.

He talked about having worked as a carpenter and how he liked to go fishing. He and Connie had no children, but they'd been enjoying retirement by traveling, until Connie got sick. Bill could not express his feelings about the fact that his wife was dying.

One day, over coffee in the cafeteria, I got him on the subject of women and how we need romance in our lives; how we love to get sentimental cards and love letters.

"Do you tell Connie you love her?" I asked (knowing his answer), and he looked at me as if I was crazy.

"I don't have to," he said. "She knows I do!"

"I'm sure she knows," I said, reaching over and touching his hands rough, carpenter's hands that were gripping the cup as if it were the only thing he had to hang onto "but she needs to hear it, Bill. She needs to hear what she has meant to you all these years. Please think about it."

We walked back to Connie's room. Bill disappeared inside, and I left to visit another patient. Later, I saw Bill sitting by the bed. He was holding Connie's hand as she slept. The date was February 12.

Two days later, I walked down the hospice ward at noon. There stood Bill,

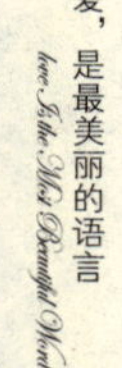

我愿意付出一切，可这根本不是他的性格。”

比尔每天都来探望康尼。起初，康尼看肥皂剧，他就坐在床旁。后来，她睡的时候多了，比尔就在屋外走廊里踱来踱去。不久，康尼不再看电视了，醒的时候也少了，我开始花更多的义工时间和比尔在一起。

他谈到他一直是个木工，他多么喜欢钓鱼。他和康尼没有孩子，但他们四处旅游，享受着退休生活，直到康尼得病。对他妻子病危这一事实，比尔无法表达他的感受。

一天，在自助餐厅喝咖啡时，我设法和比尔谈起女人这个话题，谈到生活中我们多么需要浪漫，多想收到充满柔情蜜意的卡片和情书。

“你会跟康尼说你爱她吗？”我明知故问。他瞧着我，就好像我有神经病一样。

“我没必要说，”他说道。“她知道我爱她！”

“我肯定她知道，”我说。我伸出手，触摸着他那双粗糙的木工的手。这双手紧握着杯子，似乎它是他需要依附的唯一东西——“可是她需要听到它，比尔。她需要听到所有这些年来她对你的意义。请你考虑考虑。”

我们走回康尼的房间。比尔进了屋，我走开去看望另一个病人。后来，我看见比尔坐在床边。康尼入睡了，他握着她的手。那天是 2 月 12 日。

两天后的中午时分，我顺着收容所病房过道向前走着。比尔站在那里，靠着墙，凝视着地面。护士长已经告诉我，康尼在上午 11 点故去了。

leaning up against the wall in the hallway, staring at the floor. I already knew from the head nurse that Connie had died at 11 a.m.

When Bill saw me, he allowed himself to come into my arms for a long time. His face was wet with tears and he was trembling. Finally, he leaned back against the wall and took a deep breath.

"I have to say something," he said. "I have to say how good I feel about telling her." He stopped to blow his nose. "I thought a lot about what you said, and this morning I told her how much I loved her... and loved being married to her. You should see her smile!"

I went into the room to say my own goodbye to Connie. There, on the bedside table, was a large Valentine card from Bill. You know, the sentimental kind that says, "To my wonderful wife... I love you."

比尔看见我后，让我拥抱了他许久。他满脸泪水，浑身颤抖。最后，他向后靠在墙上，深深地吸了一口气。

“我必须得说点什么，”他说道。“我得说，对她说出来，感觉真是好极了。”他停下来擤鼻子。“你说的话我想了很多；今天早上我对她说，我是多么爱她……我多么珍惜和她结为夫妻。你真该看看她的笑容！”

我走进康尼的房间，亲自去和她告别。我看见，床头桌上放着一张比尔给她的大大的情人节贺卡——你知道就是那种充满柔情蜜意的贺卡，上面写着：“给我可爱的妻子……我爱你。”

True Love

真爱

◎ Julie Parker

An ancient Hebraic text says: “love is as strong as death”. It seems that not everyone experiences this kind of strong love. The increasing poverty, crime and war tells us that the world is in indispensable need of true love. But what is true love?

Love is something we all need. But how do we know when we experience it?

True love is best seen as the devotion and action, not an emotion. Love is not exclusively based how we feel. Certainly our emotions are involved. But they cannot be our only criteria for love. True love is when you care enough about another person that you will lay down your life for them. When this happens, then love truly is as strong as death.

How many of you have a mother, or father, husband or wife, son or daughter or friend who would sacrifice his or her own life on yours? Those of you who truly love your spells but unchildren, would unselfishly lay your life on the line to save them from death? Many people in an emergency room with their loved ones and prayed “please, God, take me instead of them”.

Find true love and be a true lover as well. May you find a love which is not only strong as death, but to leave to a truly for feeling life.

美丽语录

Love is not counting the days but to make every day meaningful.

爱情不是数着日子过去，它让每个日子都变得有意义。

一篇古代希伯来文说：“爱和死一样强烈”。好像不是每个人都经历过这种强烈的爱。日益增加的贫穷、犯罪和战争告诉我们，这个世界极度需要真爱。但是，什么又是真爱？

爱是我们都需要的东西，但是我们怎么知道什么时候经历了爱？

真爱最好被看成是奉献和行动，而不是情感。爱不完全基于我们的感觉。当然，我们的情感也参与其中，但是情感不能成为我们对爱的唯一标准。真爱是当你足够关心在乎另一个人，你愿意为他们放弃自己的生命。当这一切发生时，那么爱的确是和死亡一样强烈。

你们当中有多少人的父亲或母亲、丈夫或妻子、儿女或朋友愿意为你而牺牲自己的生命？你们当中谁愿意无私地放弃自己的生命来拯救你真正爱着的配偶和孩子，拯救他们脱离死亡？许多人在急救室为他们所爱的人祈祷，“上帝，请让我来代替他们”。

找到真爱，并成为一个真正的爱人。祝愿你找到一种爱——不仅和死亡一样强烈，而且让你真正地感受生命。

爱因艰难而珍贵

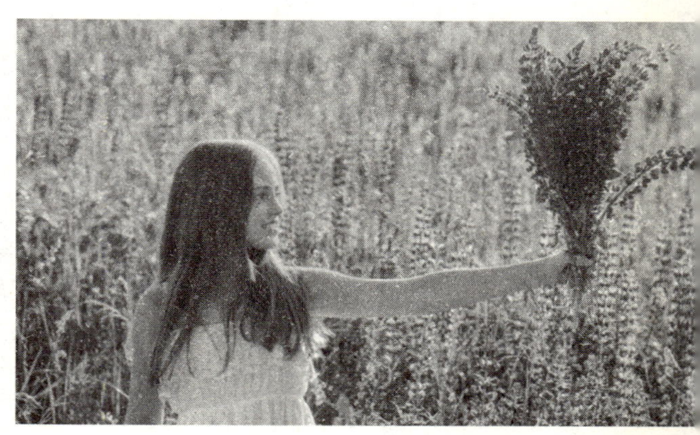

They knew that they had moved many people with their love, and they had been given the greatest gift of all. They had the gift of love. And it's never known where it will land.

他们知道，他们真挚的爱情打动了许多人，他们也因此收获了最珍贵的礼物——爱情。爱情会在哪里停歇，你永远都不会知道。

Where Love Lands

爱的港湾

© Diana Chapman

No one knows where love's wings will land. At times, it turns up in the most unusual spots. There was nothing more surprising than when it descended upon a **rehabilitation**[①] hospital in a Los Angeles suburb—a hospital where most of the patients can no longer move of their own accord.

When the staff heard the news, some of the nurses began to cry. The administrator was in shock, but from then on, Harry MacNarama would bless it as one of the greatest days in his entire life.

Now the trouble was, how were they going to make the wedding dress? He knew his staff would find a way, and when one of his nurses volunteered, Harry was relieved. He wanted this to be the finest day in the lives of two of his patients—Juana and Michael.

Michael strapped in his wheelchair and breathing through his **ventilator**[②], appeared at Harry's office door one morning.

"Harry, I want to get married," Michael announced.

"Married?" Harry's mouth dropped open. How serious was this? "To whom?" Harry asked.

"To Juana," Michael said. "We're in love."

① rehabilitation [ˌriːhəˌbiliˈteiʃən] n. 修复；恢复名誉；(病残人的)康复

② ventilator [ˈventileitə] n. 通风机，通风口；通风管

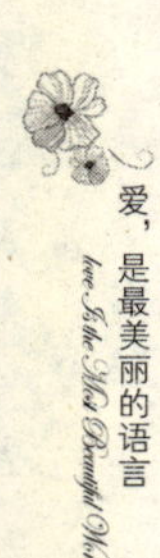

美丽语录

A person who truly loves you will never let you go, no matter how hard the situation is.

真心爱你的人永远不会放你走，不管遇到多大的困境。

爱的羽翼会在哪里停歇，没有人知道。偶尔，它会出现在最不寻常的地方。最令人难以置信的是，它出现在洛杉矶郊区的一家康复医院里——那儿的大多数病人都丧失了最基本的身体机能。

当医院的工作人员听到这个消息时，有几个护士哭了。院长震惊了，从那一刻开始，哈利把它当作人生中最伟大的日子，并为它祈祷。

现在的问题是，怎么给他们缝制结婚礼服呢？他知道他的员工会找到办法的。一个护士提出自愿效劳时，哈利放心了。他希望这将是两位病人——朱安娜和迈克一生中最美好的时光。

一天早上，迈克出现在哈利的办公室门口，他的身子用带子缚在轮椅上，还需要借助呼吸器呼吸。

“哈利，我想结婚。”迈克大声宣布。

“结婚？”哈利张大着嘴巴，他说这话是认真的吗？他接着问道：“跟谁呢？”

Love. Love had found its way through the hospital doors, over two bodies that refused to work for their owners and penetrated their hearts—despite the fact that the two patients were unable to feed or cloth themselves, required ventilators just to breath and could never walk again. Michael had spinal muscular atrophy; Juana had multiple sclerosis.

Just how serious this marriage idea was, became quite apparent when Michael pulled out the engagement ring and beamed as he hadn't done in years. In fact, the staff had never seen a kinder, sweeter Michael, who had been one of the angriest men Harry's employees had ever worked with.

The reason for Michael's anger was understandable. For twenty-five years, he had lived his life at a medical center where his mother had placed him at age nine and visited him several times a week until she died. He was always a raspy sort of guy, who cussed out his nurses routinely, but at least he felt he had family at the hospital. The patients were his friends.

There even had been a girl once who went about in a squeaky wheelchair who he was sure had eyed him. But she hadn't stayed long at the center. And after spending more than half his life there, now Michael wasn't going to get to stay either.

The center was closing, and Michael was shipped to live at the rehabilitation hospital, far from his friends and worse, far from Juana.

That's when Michael turned into a recluse. He wouldn't come out from his room. He left it dark. His friends drove more than two hours to see him. But Michael's spirits sagged so low, no one could reach him.

And then, one day, he was lying in bed when he heard a familiar creaking sound coming down the hall. It sounded like that same, ancient, squeaky

“跟朱安娜，我们相爱了。”迈克答道。

爱情。爱情穿越了医院的大门，降临在两个瘫痪的人身上，并住进他们的心里——虽然这两位病人衣食无法自理，需要借助呼吸器呼吸，再也无法行走。迈克得了骨髓肌肉萎缩症。朱安娜患了多发性硬化病。

结婚的念头究竟有多认真，当迈克拿出订婚戒指，露出多年不见的笑容时，态度就更加明显了。其实，此时的迈克是工作人员见过的最和善、最温柔的。之前他一直是公认的脾气最暴躁的人。

迈克的暴躁是可以理解的。25 年来，他一直生活在医疗中心。9 岁时，他妈妈将他送到那后，每周来看几次，直到她去世。他经常大发雷霆，常把护士赶走。但是，他始终觉得医院是他的家，病人们都是他的朋友。

曾经有个女孩，坐在咯吱作响的轮椅上。迈克以为她注意到自己了。可是她并没有在那待多久。迈克在那儿度过了大半辈子后，现在他也不想待下去了。

医疗中心要关门了，他被转到康复医院，远离了那些朋友。更糟糕的是，他远离了朱安娜。

迈克开始变得孤僻，喜欢待在黑暗的房间里，整天足不出户。他的朋友驱车两个多小时来看他，但迈克却依旧情绪低落，没有人能够走进他的心。

有一天，他躺在床上，走廊传来一阵熟悉的吱吱声。古老的轮椅咯吱作响，就像在以前他住的那个医疗中心遇见的女孩——朱安娜所坐的轮椅

wheelchair that girl, Juana, had used at the center where he used to live.

The squeaking stopped at his door, and Juana peered in and asked him to come outdoors with her. He was intrigued and from the moment he met Juana again, it was as though she breathed life back into him.

He was staring at the clouds and blue skies again. He began to participate in the hospital's recreation programs. He spent hours talking with Juana. His room was sunny and light. And then he asked Juana, who'd been living in a wheelchair since age twenty-four, if she would marry him.

Juana had already had a tough life. She was pulled out of school before finishing the third grade, because she collapsed and fell a lot. Her mother, thinking she was lazy, slapped her around. She lived in terror that her mother wouldn't want her anymore, so on the occasions when she was well enough, she cleaned house "like a little maid".

Before the age of twenty-four, like Michael, she had a tracheotomy just to breathe and that was when she was officially diagnosed with multiple sclerosis. By the time she was thirty, she had moved into a hospital with round-the-clock care.

So when Michael asked her the big question, she didn't think she could handle the pain if he was teasing.

"He told me he loved me, and I was so scared," she said. "I thought he was playing a game with me. But he told me it was true. He told me he loved me."

On Valentine's Day, Juana wore a wedding dress made of white satin, dotted with pearl beads and cut loose enough to drape around a wheelchair and a ventilator. Juana was rolled to the front of the room, assisted by Harry, who proudly gave the bride away. Her face streamed with tears.

发出的声音。

那个吱吱声在他的门口停住了，朱安娜盯着他，问他能否和她一起外出。他立即兴奋起来，再次见到她的那一刻，他的生命似乎重新被她带了回来。

他再次仰望蓝天白云，参加医院的娱乐活动。他会花上好几个小时和朱安娜聊天。他的房间充满了阳光和欢笑。于是，他向从 24 岁时就在轮椅上生活的朱安娜求婚，问她是否愿意和自己一起生活。

朱安娜也曾有过一段艰辛的日子。还没念完三年级，她就被赶出了学校，只因她身体虚弱很容易晕倒。妈妈以为她偷懒，老是打她。她生活在恐惧中，总是担心妈妈会抛弃自己。所以，身体好些时，她就“像个小女佣似的”打扫房间。

24 岁之前，她和迈克一样经历过一次气管切开手术，只是为了让呼吸更顺畅。也就是在那个时候，她被确诊患有多发性硬化症。30 岁时，她就被送进医院接受全天 24 小时的护理。

所以，当迈克问她这个“重大”问题时，她想，如果他只是戏弄自己的话，对她来说那将是无法忍受的痛苦。

“他说爱我时，我非常害怕，”她说，“我想他是跟我开玩笑。但是他告诉我，他是认真的，他爱我。”

情人节那天，朱安娜穿着一件白色的绸缎婚纱，上面缀着珍珠。婚纱很大，足以盖住轮椅和呼吸器。哈利自豪地把她推到房门前，她激动地泪流满面。

Michael wore a crisp white shirt, black jacket and a bow tie that fit neatly over his tracheotomy. He beamed with pleasure.

Nurses filled the doorways. Patients filled the room. An overflow of hospital employees spilled into the halls. Sobs echoed in every comer of the room. In the hospital's history, no two people—living their lives bound to wheelchairs—had ever married.

Janet Yamaguchi, the hospital's recreation leader, had planned everything. Employees had donated their own money to buy the red and white balloons, matching flowers, and an archway dotted with leaves. Janet had the hospital chef make a three-tiered, lemon-filled wedding cake. A marketing consultant hired a photographer.

Janet negotiated with family members. It was one of the most trying and satisfying times of her life to watch the couple get married.

She thought of everything.

The final touch—the kiss—could not be completed. Janet used a white **satin**[①] rope to tie the couple's wheelchairs to symbolize the romantic moment.

After the ceremony, the minister slipped out trying to hold back her tears. "I've performed thousands of weddings, but this is the most wonderful one I've done so far," the minister said. "These people have passed the barriers and showed pure love."

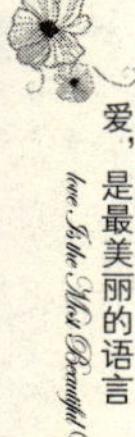

That evening, Michael and Juana rolled into their own room for the first time together. Michael and Juana knew they had moved many people with their love, and they had been given the greatest gift of all. They had the gift of love. And it's never known where it will land.

① satin ['sætin] n. 缎；缎子衣服

迈克穿着笔挺的白衬衣和黑夹克，动了手术的脖子上还打了一个精美的蝴蝶结，脸上洋溢着幸福的微笑。

护士和病人挤满了走廊、房间，甚至连医院的大厅都挤满了医护人员。房间的每个角落里都能听到哽咽声。医院有史以来，还没有两个生活在轮椅上的人结合的先例。

医院的娱乐带头人珍妮特早已安排好了一切活动。医护人员用捐来的钱买了红色、白色的气球，树叶缠绕的拱门上插满了鲜花。珍妮特请医院的厨师做了一个三层高的柠檬味的婚礼蛋糕。一个市场营销顾问还请来了摄影师。

珍妮特和家人谈起这件事情。看着这对有情人终成眷属，是她这辈子最下功夫、最满意的时刻。

她考虑到了所有事情。

最后的程序——接吻——无法完成。珍妮特用一根白色绸缎将两人的轮椅绑在一起，以象征这个浪漫时刻。

婚礼结束后，牧师强忍着泪水走了出去。“我主持过成千上万次的婚礼，但这次是最激动人心的。牧师说，“这些人跨过了障碍，寻得了最纯洁的爱情。”

那天晚上，迈克和朱安娜一齐步入他们的新房。他们知道，他们真挚的爱情打动了许多人，他们也因此收获了最珍贵的礼物——爱情。爱情会在哪里停歇，你永远都不会知道。

My One and Only

我的唯一

◎ Keith Green

It was all started when I was in high school, I still remember my love one. I am not sure if it is puppy love or first love, but I know deep inside my heart that I still remember him.

At first we were bus mate, and schoolmate too. I was in 1st year high school and he was in second. We still don't know each other before, but later on when I was sitting in front of him in the bus, he used to talk and tease me, which makes me angry with him. I used to say that I hate him but later on... I only eat my words. One day when my best friend wanted to see what I wrote in my diary, I was reading it in the bus and without noticing the guy whom I hate was sitting back of me with his buddies. He was peeping and reading the things what I wrote in the diary. I looked sharply at him and put the book down, then my friend who was in front of me that she has read what I wrote there that love is BOG, BOG, BOG in my heart. He was hearing it and suddenly without my knowledge he stood and snatched the diary from me! Whew! What he did was to read the book so loudly where everything was written there about love! Goodness! I was so shocked that I was screaming just to get it back. I couldn't believe it, because

美丽语录

Grasp the happiness around it, don't let it slip away.

把握身边的幸福吧，不要让它擦肩而过。

一切开始于我的高中时代，直到现在我还记得他。我无法确定那是孩子间不成熟的恋情还是我的初恋。但我知道，在我的内心深处，我依然无法将他忘记。

起初，我们只是同校，和搭乘同一路公车的路友。我上高一，他上高二。之前，我们并不认识对方。但是，后来，坐在公车上，我坐在他的前面，他经常会拿话题取笑我，这让我十分气恼。我曾经说过讨厌他，不过后来……我食言了。一天，我最好的朋友想要看看我的日记里都写些什么，于是我就在公车上读起了我在日记本里写的东西。当然，我不知道我厌恶的那个男孩和他的一群兄弟就坐在我的后面。他偷看我写的内容。我狠狠地瞪了他一眼，赶快把日记本放下。这时，坐在我前面的好友说她读完我写的东西后觉得爱情在我心中就是“泥潭、沼泽、令人动弹不得”。那个男孩听到这句话，在我不知道的情况下突然站起来把我的日记本抢走了！天呐！他正在大声朗读我写的内容，日记本上写的都是关于爱情的内容！天啊！我太震惊了，尖叫着把日记本抢了回来，我简直不敢相信，因为他就

he's the most intelligent student in my school and he's the **representative**① of our school too. Then after the bus dropped me to my house there I felt that I was so flushing hotly that my cheeks were so red! There, I realized that I have a crush on him!

Sports date came, and he was the champion for C group boys for running. Whew! Wow! I was really amazed when he runs, because he always come first in running and he runs like a wind. That day I felt more feelings for him. I used to write him always in my diary, but mostly he always went to another place because of interschool **quiz**②.

I cried that time, because I was missing him so much, that I wish one day he'll like me too. Then one day I just heard that he likes me! My god, I nearly faint! Rumors spread that in the bus we always fights for simple things like teasing, because I use to call him nutcracker which makes him so mad at me, and I always teased him for his pimples and about his using facial cleanser which made my whole bus mates burst out laughing, and he was blushing, and then one fine day the rumors spread that we both are loving each other! Whenever we cross our paths we just look each other casually, but my hearts beats fast because he looks at me so intensely which makes my heart tremble. I used to be always so naughty that time. One day I decided to ask my friend to write a love letter in language of German I loved, since we both are from different nations.

My friend wrote it, and in the bus I asked him to read the letter for me. He read it and explained what was written, and I know the last word written there was just I love you, but he told me that the last word means "I love you" which

① representative [repri'zentətiv] adj. 典型的，代表的；代理的

② quiz [kwiz] n. 考查，测验；挖苦，戏弄者

是全校最聪明的学生，并且还是学校的学生代表。汽车停下后，我连忙赶回家，我浑身发热，两颊也变得通红了。就是那个时候，我意识到自己有点喜欢他！

运动会开始了，他获得了C组男子组短跑冠军。天啊！哇！他经常获得跑步冠军，他的跑步速度飞快，就像一阵风似的，这点真的让我很惊奇。那天，我对他又多了一些感觉。我还常常在日记中提到他。可他经常不在学校，因为他参加了许多校际竞赛。

有一次，我因为太想他而哭了起来。我多么希望有一天他也会喜欢上我。一天，我居然听别人说他喜欢我！我的天啊，我差点晕了过去！以前，大家总说我们因为一些鸡毛蒜皮的小事，比如讥讽而在公车上大声争吵。因为我常常叫他“坚果钳”，这使他很不高兴。我常常取笑他因为脸上的粉刺而用洗面奶，这使得全车的人听后都捧腹大笑，他的脸唰的一下就红了。突然有一天，居然传出了我们彼此喜欢对方的谣言！无论什么时候走过街头，我们也只是偶尔互望一下，但是我的心跳加速了，因为他正在用一种强烈的目光看着我，这也让我的心开始颤抖。那时，我一直很调皮。有一天，我决定让我的朋友用我喜欢的德语写一封情书，因为，我们俩不是来自同一个国家。

我的朋友真的写了一封情书。于是，在公车上，我让他把这封情书念给我听。他读了，并向我解释了信的内容。我知道情书最后一句话写的是“我爱你”。他念到那时，他就告诉我那几个字的意思是“我爱你”。这句话

makes me blushed! Oh even though I know that he wasn't the one who wrote it, but it seems like he is telling it from his heart!

But not all the love story has happy ending...

One day, I heard that he likes another girl which makes my heart break! In the bus, I used to make him jealous of me by saying that I have a boyfriend. I made it, and he was jealous! Then examination came. I was really broken-heart when I saw him waiting for a girl in the gate! I cried, because of his caring for dating girl. Five days before the exam came, he told me in the bus that he's going to his country! My god! I can't believe it he's leaving me! The last day in the school and in the bus, I took a picture of him in my own camera! And when he went down in the bus I told bye... and then I still can't believe that he's gone.

To tell you we both are in the same bus, same school, we both are born on the same year. That was HAMLET! By Shakespeare I was the dancer, and he's Hamlet. I can never forget my one, my only one. He dreamed about me so many times! He even include the poem A KISS IN THE RAIN in his dream and we both composed a poem for each other, I composed a poem for him "ONLY YOU", and he composed a poem for me "SHE'S MINE". I still can't forget the happy unforgettable moments once we shared! Oh, **nostalgia**[①]—

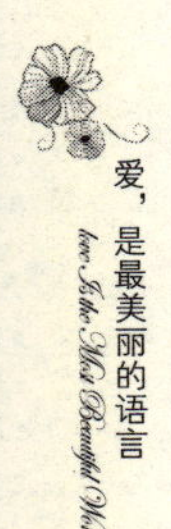

① nostalgia [nɔs'tældʒiə] n. 乡愁；怀旧之情

让我面红耳赤！虽然我知道这封情书不是他写的，但那仿佛就是他的心声！

然而，不是所有的爱情故事都能有个美好结局……

一天，我听说他喜欢上了另一个女孩，我的心碎了！在公车上，为了让他嫉妒，我就撒谎说自己有个男朋友。我撒了谎，他真的嫉妒了！接下来，又该考试了。当我看见他在学校门口等一个女孩时，我的心彻底地碎了！我哭了，因为他那么在乎和他约会的女孩。考试开始的五天前，他在公车上告诉我，他很快就要回国了！天呐！我简直不敢相信他要离开我了！最后一天在学校和公车上遇见他时，我用自己的相机拍下了他的照片！当他下车时，我只说了声“再见”……我还是无法相信他要离开了。

告诉你们吧！我们上同一所学校，坐同一路公交，在同一年出生。他就是哈姆雷特！在莎士比亚的作品中，我是那位舞者，他就是哈姆雷特。我永远不会忘记我的唯一。他也曾多次梦见我！甚至那首诗《雨中一吻》也在他的梦中出现。我们为彼此写了一首诗：我给他写了一首诗，题为《唯一》；他为我写了一首诗，名为《她是我的》。我依旧无法忘记那些幸福的、难以忘怀的我们一起度过的美好时光。噢！怀念美好的往昔——

如意郎君

◎ Lynn M. Lombard

When I was younger, I used to dream of finding Mr. Right.

After each heartbreak, I would wonder how long it would take me to find him. I didn't realize it then, but each relationship taught me a lesson and brought me one step closer to true love. It went something like this:

Tony and I walked down Bloomingdale Avenue holding hands. His friend was with us and suggested we kiss goodbye. I said okay. Tony's eyes became the size of golf balls, "I can't believe you said that!" (And not because he was not looking forward to the kiss). So with one quick peck on his lips, I headed for home. When I dumped him a few weeks later, I thought he was going to hate me for life. He tattled on me to the teacher each chance he got, making me cry and look like a baby in gym class. Tony taught me that boys can be jerks, even bigger ones if you break their heart.

In seventh grade, I had a crush on Billy. His hair was longer than mine, and he was missing a few front teeth, but each time he smiled at me, I melted. With a locker right next to mine, he would pick on me everyday, but I never quite got the hint that there was no future for us. What did Billy teach me? He taught me

美丽语录

One day someone walk into your life, then you will realize that love is always worth waiting for.

当某天某个人走进你生命时，你就会明白，真爱总是值得等待的。

当我还是个小女孩的时候，就常常梦想着有一天能找到我的如意郎君。

可每次经历过失恋的痛苦后，我总在想，自己到底何时才能找到我的他啊！然而，那时的我还未意识到，我的每一段恋情都教会了我一些东西，并使我向真爱更靠近了一步。事情是这样的：

我和托尼手牵着手漫步在布卢明黛尔大街。那个时候，他的朋友也跟我们一起，他提议让我们吻别。我说当然可以啊！这时，托尼的眼睛睁得像高尔夫球那么大，他说道："我简直不敢相信你同意了！"（他如此惊讶并不是因为他不想和我吻别）。于是，我在他的嘴唇上迅速地亲了一下，就朝家里走去。几个星期后，我甩了他。我想他会因此恨我一辈子的。果然，从那以后，只要一有机会，他就会向老师打我的小报告。我因此大哭了一场，仿佛自己成了一个不愿上体育课的小孩。托尼让我明白：男孩，即使是大男孩，如果你伤了他们的心，他们也会打击报复的。

七年级的时候，我喜欢上了比利。他的头发比我的还长，还掉了几颗

that no matter how much you **drool**[1] over a guy, it won't make him drool back.

In tenth grade, I fell for a guy who had **previously**[2] shown interest in my sister. How stupid is that? He came over to my house a few times, hardly talking to me at all as he sat there in my family room. We would write each other notes in school, the scent of his cologne lingering on each letter. Not long after, my sister began to like him too. He was the one and only guy we fought over. What he taught me was invable—no guy is worth two sisters fighting.

My first "real" kiss happened with an out-of-town boyfriend, whom I didn't see very often. When I realized I didn't like him quite as much as he liked me, I dumped him over the phone (what a heartbreaker I was!) and cried because I felt so bad. I learned form that relationship that if one like the other more, it will never work.

After all these lessons, I had doubts that I would ever find Mr. Right.

But a year later, I was reacquainted with a man whose smile and kind words always flattered me back in high school. When we saw one another at a graduation party on a rainy, warm night in July, I felt my heart skip a beat. Somehow, I knew he was the one. We instantly found ourselves comfortable with each other and my doubts were put to rest.

I'll never forget the day when we were sitting in my driveway in his truck, saying our goodbyes after spending the day together. Doug put his hand on my cheek and in a serious tone, said, "Someday, I'm going to marry you." I had no doubt that he was right. Today I share his last name and I couldn't be happier.

When I think back to Tony, Billy, and the rest of the boys, I smile. If I was

---

① drool [dru:l] vi. 流口水；胡说

② previously ['pri:vjəsli] adv. 事先；以前

门牙，可每次他冲着我微笑时，我仿佛在顷刻间被他融化了。我们的储物箱紧挨着，他每天都会拿我开玩笑。可我还是没有醒悟过来，我们之间是没有未来的。那么，比利又教会了我什么呢？他让我明白：无论你对一个男孩多么痴心，也无法让他用同样的痴心对你。

十年级的时候，我爱上了一个对我的姐姐感兴趣的男生。这是不是很愚蠢？他来过我家几次，但他就坐在我家的家庭活动室里，没跟我说过一句话。在学校里，我们会互传小纸条。他身上那股淡淡的古龙香水味停留在了每一封信上。不久之后，我的姐姐也开始喜欢他了。他成了唯一一个让我们姐妹争得死去活来的男孩。他让我明白了：不管什么样的男人，都不值得我们姐妹俩为他争风吃醋。

我“真正”的初吻献给了一个外地的男朋友。我们俩不经常见面。当我意识到他喜欢我胜过我喜欢他时，我就在电话里甩了他（我太残忍了！），而我也伤心地大哭了一场，只因那样做让我感觉很糟糕。这段恋情让我懂得：如果一个人付出的比对方多得多，那么这段恋情也是不会有结果的。

经历了这么多教训后，我开始怀疑自己能否找到属于我的如意郎君。

然而，一年后，我和一个家伙再次相遇了。高中时，他的迷人微笑和善意话语总能打动我的心。在七月的一个温和多雨的夜晚，我们在毕业舞会上相遇了。刹那间，我感觉到自己的心跳停顿了一下。说不出是什么原因，我觉得他就是我要找的如意郎君。我们很快便发现彼此相处得很融洽。我心中的那个疑问也随风消逝了。

我永远忘不了那一天，我们在一起度过了一整天后，我们坐在他的卡车里道别，他的车就停在我家的车道上。道格抚摸着我的脸，十分严肃地说道：“总有一天，我会娶你的。”他是认真的，这点我从来不曾怀疑过。如今，我和他姓着同样的姓，过着幸福无比的生活。

当我回想起托尼、比利还有其他我爱过的男孩时，我笑了。如果我能

able to go back and change a thing, I wouldn't. Each relationship was an essential part of my life, there to teach me a thing or two about love. It also taught me that it's okay to be picky about the people you date. Finding Mr. Right takes patience.

And I'm the proof that good things come to those who wait.

回到从前，并且有能力改变我的过去，我不愿意去改。每一次的情感经历都是我生命中不可或缺的部分，是它们教会了我一些关于爱情的道理；是它们让我明白，对与你交往的人挑剔一些也是正确的。寻找如意郎君需要耐心。

好事多磨，而我就很好地证明了这个道理。

Appointment with Love
爱的约会

◎ S. L Kishor

Six minutes to six, said the clock over the information booth in New York's Grand Central Station. The tall, young Army **lieutenant**① lifted his sunburned face and narrowed his eyes to note the exact time. His heart was pounding with a beat. In six minutes he would see the woman who had filled such a special place in his life for the past 13 months, the woman he had never seen, yet whose written words had sustained him unfailingly.

Lieutenant Blandford remembered one day in particular, during the worst of the fighting, when his plane had been caught in the midst of a pack of enemy planes. In one of his letters he had confessed to her that he often felt fear, and only a few days before this battle he had received her answer, "Of course you fear... all brave men do. Next time you doubt yourself, I want you to hear my voice reciting to you, 'yeah, though I walk through the Valley of the Shadow of Death, I will fear no evil: for thou art with me.'..." He had remembered, and it had renewed his strength.

Now he was going to hear her real voice. Four minutes to six.

① lieutenant [lef'tenənt] n.（美国）陆军中尉，少尉；副职官员

美丽语录

With the most true to myself, to meet the most should be that person.
用最真实的自己，才能遇见最应该的那个人。

在纽约的地铁中心总站，问讯处上方的时钟显示的时间是5点54分。年轻高大的陆军中尉抬起黝黑的脸庞，眯起眼睛注意着那上面的确切时间。他的心激动地怦怦直跳。再过6分钟，他就能见到那个女人了——一个在过去的13个月占据了他心中某个特殊位置的女人。虽然他们素未谋面，但是她的信一直是支撑他的精神支柱。

布兰德福中尉还记得那一天，那是战斗最艰苦的时刻，他的飞机被敌机重重包围。他曾在一封信中向她坦白，他经常感到畏惧。就在战斗打响的前几天，他收到了她的回信："当然你会感到畏惧……所有勇敢的人都会那样。下次你再怀疑自己的时候，我希望你能听到我为你朗诵的声音：'啊，虽然我要走过死亡之谷，但是我将勇往直前，因为你与我同在。'……"他记得，就是这封信让他重新振作的。

现在，他很快就能听到她真实的声音了，还差4分钟就6点了。

一个女孩朝他走来，布兰德福中尉一惊。女孩戴着一朵花，但却不是

A girl passed close to him, and Lieutenant Blandford stared. She was wearing a flower, but it was not the little red rose they had agreed upon. Besides, this girl was only about 18, and Hollis Meynell had told him she was 30. "What of it?" he had answered. "I'm 32." He was 29.

His mind went back to that book he had read in the training camp. Of Human Bondage it was; and throughout the book were notes in a woman's handwriting. He had never believed that a woman could see into a man's heart so **tenderly**[①], so understandingly. Her name was on the book plate: Hollis Meynell. He had got hold of a New York City telephone book and found her address. He had written; she had answered. Next day he had been shipped out, but they had gone on writing.

For 13 months she had faithfully replied. When his letters did not arrive, she wrote anyway, and now he believed that he loved her and that she loved him.

But she had refused all his pleas to send him her photograph. She had explained, "If your feeling for me has any reality, what I look like won't matter. Suppose I'm beautiful. I'd always be haunted by the feeling that you had been taking a chance on just that, and that kind of love would disgust me. Suppose I'm plain (and you must admit that this is more likely), then I'd always fear that you were only going on writing because you were lonely and had no one else. No, don't ask for my picture. When you come to New York, you shall see me and then you shall make your decision."

One minute to six ... he pulled hard on a cigarette. Then Lieutenant Blandford's heart leaped.

A young woman was coming toward him. Her figure was long and slim;

① tenderly ['tendəli] adv. 温和地，柔和地，可怜地

他们约定好的那种红色玫瑰花。她只有 18 岁的样子，而霍丽斯·梅内尔告诉过他，她已经 30 岁了。“有什么关系呢？”他还回信说，“我已经 32 岁。”而其实他才 29 岁。

他想起了在训练营里看过的一本书——《人性的枷锁》，书里有一个女人写满了批注。他简直不敢相信，一个女人能如此温和如此透彻地读懂男人的心。她的名字就写在书签上——霍丽斯·梅内尔。于是，他找来一本纽约市的电话簿，查到了地址，给她写了信，并收到了回信。因为第二天他要执行任务，就乘船离开了，可是他们还是保持通信。

在过去的 13 个月里，她始终真挚地给他回信。常常他的信还没到，她的信就来了。因此，他相信，他们彼此深爱着对方。

可是，她一直拒绝送他照片，并曾解释说：“如果你是真心爱我，那我的外表就不再重要了。如果我长得很漂亮，我会认为，你爱的只是我的外表，那会令我很反感。如果我相貌平平（你必须承认这个可能性更大），那我便会担心，你和我通信只是因为内心孤独，无人倾诉。别向我要照片。你来纽约时就能见到我了，到时再做决定也不迟。”

还差 1 分钟就 6 点了，布兰德福猛吸了一口烟，心跳得更快了。

一位年轻的女士向他走来，她身材苗条，金黄的卷发散落在小巧的耳朵旁。她的双唇红润，下巴精致，一双蓝色的眼眸像花儿一样美丽。她穿着淡绿色的西装，浑身散发出一股青春的气息。

her blond hair lay back in curls over her delicate ears. Her eyes were as blue as flowers, her lips and chin had a gentle firmness. In her pale-green suit, she was like springtime come alive.

He stared toward her, forgetting to notice that she was wearing no rose, and as he moved, a small, provocative smile curved her lips.

"Going my way, soldier?" she murmured. He made one step closer to her. Then he saw Hollis Meynell.

She was standing almost directly behind the girl, a woman well past 40, her graying hair tucked under a worn hat. She was more than **plump**[①]; her thick ankled feet were thrust into low-heeled shoes.

But she wore a red rose on her rumpled coat. The girl in the green suit was walking quickly. Blandford felt as though he were being split into two, so keen was his desire to follow the girl, yet so deep was his longing for the woman whose spirit had truly companioned and upheld his own; and there she stood. He could see her pale, plump face was gentle and sensible; her gray eyes had a warm twinkle.

Lieutenant Blandford did not hesitate. His fingers gripped the worn copy of Human Bondage which was to identify him to her. This would not be love, but it would be something precious, a friendship for which he had been and must ever be grateful...

He squared his shoulders, saluted, and held the book out toward the woman, although even while he spoke he felt the bitterness of his disappointment. "I'm John Blandford, and you—you are Miss Meynell. May—may I take you to dinner?"

① plump [plʌmp] adj. 丰满的；多肉的；凸起的

他朝她望去，一时忘了她并没有戴红色玫瑰花。他走近，发现她的嘴角露出动人的微笑。

“问路吗，军人？”她嘀咕着说。他又走近了一步，这时，他看到了霍丽斯·梅内尔。

霍丽斯·梅内尔就站在这位年轻女士的身后，一个40多岁的女人，灰白的头发塞在一顶破旧的帽子下面，很胖，厚实的双脚上穿着一双低跟鞋。

可是她那皱巴巴的外套上别了一朵红色玫瑰花。穿着淡绿色西装的年轻女孩匆匆离去了。布兰德福感觉自己的心被撕成了两半，他多想跟着那个年轻的女孩啊，可是他又渴望见到这个女人，毕竟是她的精神一直陪伴着他，鼓励着他。现在，她就站在那儿，苍白丰满的面庞，温柔而理性，灰色的眼里闪烁着温和的光芒。

布兰福德中尉没有犹豫，他抓紧那本破旧的《人性的枷锁》，那是用来向她表明身份用的。尽管这不会是爱，却是一种珍贵的东西，是他曾经拥有并要感激的友情。

尽管因为深深的失望而痛苦，他还是摆正双肩，敬了个礼，然后把那本书递给她，“我是约翰·布兰德福，您——您是梅内尔小姐吧？我能——能请你吃顿饭吗？”

The woman smiled. “I don’t know what this is all about, son,” she answered. “That young lady in the green suit, she begged me to wear this rose on my coat. And she said that if you asked me to go out with you, I should tell you she’s waiting for you in that restaurant across the street. She said it was some kind of a test.”

那个女人笑着答道："孩子，我不知道这是怎么回事，那位穿绿西装的年轻小姐请求我把这朵红色的玫瑰花戴在外套上。她说如果你邀请我一起出去，就告诉你，她在街对面的那家餐厅等着你。她说，这是一种考验。"

爱是艰难的

© Rainer Maria Rilke

It is also good to love: because love is difficult. For one human being to love another human being: that is perhaps the most difficult task that has been **entrusted**① to us, the ultimate task, the final test and proof, the work for which all other work is merely preparation. That is why young people, who are beginners in everything, are not yet capable of love: it is something they must learn. With their whole being, with all their forces, gathered around their solitary, anxious, upward-beating heart, they must learn to love. But learning-time is always a long, secluded time ahead and far on into life, is solitude, a heightened and deepened kind of aloneness for the person who loves. Loving does not at first mean **merging**②, surrendering, and uniting with another person (for what would a union be of two people who are unclarified, unfinished, and still incoherent). It is a high **inducement**③ for the individual to ripen, to become something in himself, to become world, to become world in himself for the sake of another person; it is a great, demanding claim on him, something that chooses him and calls him

① entrust [in'trʌst] v. 委托；托管

② merge [mə:dʒ] v. 使合并；使融合

③ inducement [in'dju:smənt] n. 引诱，劝诱；诱因，动机

美丽语录

Be careful... When you give your heart to someone, you also give that person the power to hurt you.

谨慎一点吧……当你把你的心给某个人，你也给了这个人伤害你的能力。

这对爱来说是件好事：因为爱也是艰难的。因为让一个人去爱另一个人，这也许是上帝指派给我们的最重大、最艰巨的首要任务，是最后的考验和证明，别的工作只不过是为此而作的准备罢了。这就是为什么一切还刚刚开始的年轻人无法去爱。他们必须先学习什么是爱，用他们的整个生命，用他们的所有力量，用积聚了他们的孤独、焦虑和充满荣誉感的心去学习爱。然而，在这个长久而专注的学习过程中，爱会永远镌刻在你的生命中——在深深的寂寞中孤独地等待，只是为了那个所爱的人。爱的涵义不是倾心、献身以及与他人结合（对于一个懵懂的、涉世不深的、办事无条理的人来说，那会是怎样的一种结合呢？）。爱是一种诱惑力，它吸引着人们去成熟，去完善自己，去成就世界，为了另一个人去充实自己；爱是一种伟大而艰巨的要求，是它选择了一个人，并呼唤着他走向远方。如此

to vast distances. Only in this sense, as the task of working on themselves ("to hearken and to hammer day and night"), may young people use the love that is given to them. Merging and surrendering and every kind of communion is not for them (who must still, for a long, long time, save and gather themselves); it is the ultimate, is perhaps that for which human lives are as yet barely large enough.

看来，年轻人必须把爱看作是他们的工作（“日夜不分的敲打、锤炼”），希望他们能够善用那些赐予他们的爱。倾心、献身以及每一种结合都不是为他们而准备的（他们还需要很长很长时间的克制和积累）；因为那是爱的最高境界，是人类目前几乎无法达到的境界。

Salty Coffee

咸咖啡

◎ Trinity Bluce

He met her at a party. She was outstanding, many guys were after her; but nobody paid any attention to him. After the party, he invited her for coffee. She was surprised, so as not to appear rude, she went along. As they sat in a nice coffee shop, he was too nervous to say anything and she felt uncomfortable. Suddenly, he asked the waiter, "Could you please give me some salt? I'd like to put it in my coffee."

They stared at him. He turned red, but when the salt came, he put it in his coffee and drank. **Curious**[①], she asked, "Why salt with coffee?" He explained, "When I was a little boy, I lived near the sea. I liked playing on the sea... I could feel its taste salty, like salty coffee. Now every time I drink it, I think of my childhood and my hometown. I miss it and my parents, who are still there."

She was deeply touched. A man who can admit that he's **homesick**[②] must love his home and care about his family. He must be responsible.

She talked too, about her faraway hometown, her childhood, her family.

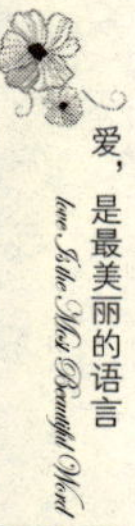

① curious ['kjuəriəs] adj. 好奇的，渴望知道的；稀奇古怪的

② homesick ['həumsik] adj. 怀乡病的，思家的

美丽语录

Love is not the strong vow but the simple accompany.

爱情不是轰轰烈烈的誓言，而是平平淡淡的陪伴。

他在一个聚会上遇见了她。她如此出众，许多人都追随她左右，而他又是如此普通，没人注意到他。聚会结束后，他邀请她喝咖啡，她很惊讶，但出于礼貌她还是应允了。他们坐在一家很不错的咖啡店，他紧张地说不出话来，她感到很不舒服。突然，他问服务员，“你能给我一些盐吗？我想往咖啡里加点盐。”

每个人都很诧异地盯着他，这人太奇怪了。他的脸红了，但是服务生把盐送来时，他还是把盐加进了咖啡里，喝了起来。她很好奇，便问道：“你为什么有这个嗜好？”他解释说，“当我还是一个小男孩的时候，我住在海边。我喜欢在海边玩耍……我可以感觉到海水的味道，就像加盐的咖啡一样。现在每次喝咸咖啡的时候，我总会想起我的童年，我的故乡。我很想念我的家乡，我的父母，他们还在那里。”

她被深深地感动了。那是他的真情流露。一个能告诉别人乡愁的男人，

That was the start to their love story.

They continued to date. She found that he met all her requirements. He was tolerant, kind, warm and careful. And to think she would have missed the catch if not for the salty coffee!

So they married and lived happily together. And every time she made coffee for him, she put in some salt, the way he liked it.

After 40 years, he passed away and left her a letter which said:

My dearest, please forgive my life-long lie. Remember the first time we dated? I was so nervous I asked for salt instead of sugar.

It was hard for me to ask for a change, so I just went ahead. I never thought that we would hit it off. Many times, I tried to tell you the truth, but I was afraid that it would ruin everything.

Sweetheart, I don't exactly like salty coffee. But as it mattered so much to you, I've learnt to enjoy it. Having you with me was my greatest happiness. If I could live a second time, I hope we can be together again, even if it means that I have to drink salty coffee for the rest of my life.

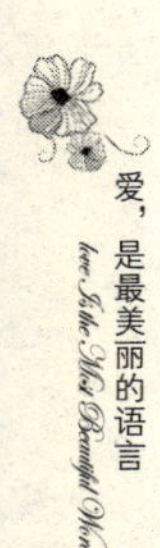

一定是一个爱家、关心家人、有家庭责任感的男人。

接着，她也开始说起了她遥远的家乡，她的童年，她的家人。那真是一个温馨的谈话，也是他们之间故事的开端。

接着他们又约会。她发现他真是一个能够满足自己所有要求的男人。他耐心、善良、热心、细心。这是一个好男人，可她就差点错过了。多亏了那杯咸咖啡！

他们结婚了，幸福地生活在一起。每次她为他煮咖啡，都会往里面放些盐，因为他喜欢。

40 年后，他去世了，留给她一封信：

我最亲爱的，请原谅我一生的谎言。记得我们的第一次约会吗？我很紧张，紧张到问服务员要了盐而不是糖。

我很难要求更改，所以我就这样喝了。我从来没有想到我们会合得来。很多次，我想告诉你真相，但是我怕那会毁了一切。

亲爱的，我不喜欢咸咖啡。但这对你来说那么重要，我已经学会了享受它。拥有你是我最大的幸福。如果我能再活一次，我希望我们还能在一起，即使这意味着我的余生都要品尝咸咖啡。

A Moving Letter to My Wife
写给在天堂的妻子

© Frank Fields

When Christian Spragg's wife Joanne gave birth they were full of excitement... until she died just hours later. In a moving letter, Christian tells why he'll make sure their daughter Ilaria knows all about her mum.

My darling Joanne,

I still remember the conversation we had just a month before our baby daughter Ilaria was born.

Out of the blue you asked me how I'd look after her if anything happened to you. I remember telling you not to be silly but you were serious. "I'd just want you to tell her often how much her mummy loved her," you said.

"And to tell her what sort of person I was. And make sure she's clean and tidy and eats her vegetables!" Now I'm so glad we had that conversation. And I hope I've done things as you wanted.

I just wish with all my heart that you were here to enjoy all the special moments we've shared since you were taken from us.

The memories of our time together are so treasured for me now.

You used to laugh when I said I fell in love with you the moment we met

美丽语录

Relationships don't need promises, terms &conditions. It just needs two people: who can trust and who can understand.

感情不需要诺言、协议与条件。它只需要两个人：一个能够信任的人，与一个愿意理解的人。

克里斯琴·斯普拉格的妻子乔安娜生下女儿的那一刻，夫妻俩都十分激动……直到几个小时后他的妻子去世。在这封感人的信中，克里斯琴讲述了为什么一定要把关于她妈妈的一切告诉他们的女儿伊拉里娅。

我亲爱的乔安娜：

我还记得我们宝贝女儿伊拉里娅出生前一个月我们的对话。

你突然问我，如果你出了什么事，我该如何照顾我们的女儿。我记得我叫你别说傻话，可你还是一脸严肃地对我说："我只要你时常告诉她，她的妈妈有多爱她。"

"还要告诉她我是一个怎样的人。要保证她每天都是干净整洁的，还要多吃蔬菜！"现在，我很庆幸我们有过那样的对话，我希望我能做到你要我做的事。

我衷心地希望你能和我们一起分享这些特殊时刻，那些你走之后我们一起分享的时刻。

but I did. I saw you in a nightclub and finally gathered the courage to ask if you'd like a drink. I couldn't believe my luck when you said yes.

I asked you to be my wife in Venice.

We splashed out on a gondola ride, **giggling**① to ourselves. I remember you tilted your head up to the sun and told me that this was one of the best days of your life. And when you walked down the aisle I knew I'd married my soulmate, "the one".

When we found out you were pregnant we were **ecstatic**② and soon we discovered it was a girl and spent the months running up to the birth getting the nursery ready.

Every time our baby kicked you'd grab my hand, put it on your tummy and say, "Can you feel her, Christian? She's so lively!"

You wanted to call our daughter Ilaria after a family friend you'd met in Venice. You found out that in Latin it meant "always happy."

We saw Ilaria before she was born. We had a 3D scan where you can see your baby's face—she was beautiful.

I am so thankful we did that now. When you went two weeks past your due date the hospital near our home in Bolton wanted to induce you. It's hard for me to think straight about what happened next.

When Ilaria was ready to come the midwife told you to push but Ilaria's heartbeat dropped—she was in distress.

You looked at me in terror as we were surrounded by doctors trying to get Ilaria out. When she was born she was blue and nurses rushed her to the special

① giggle ['gigl] v. 咯咯地笑；傻笑

② ecstatic [ek'stæik] adj. 狂喜的；着迷的；入神的

现在，那些我们的共同记忆对我来说是多么的珍贵啊！

当我说我对你一见钟情时，你总是会哈哈大笑，但我确实是那样的。我在一家夜店见到你，最后，我终于鼓起勇气问你可否请你喝一杯。当你说愿意时，我简直不敢相信，自己居然这么幸运。

我在威尼斯向你求的婚。

我们驾着尖尖的小船行驶在威尼斯，我们尽情挥霍，开怀大笑。我记得你昂着头看着太阳说这是你一生中最美好的日子。当你走下走廊时，我知道自己娶的是一个灵魂伴侣，“我的唯一”。

当我们发现你怀孕了，我们是那样的狂喜。不久后，我们发现是个女儿，于是我们花了好几月的时间为分娩做准备，甚至都把托儿所安排好了呢！

每一次我们的宝宝踢你的时候，你都会把我的手放在你的肚子上，并对我说：“克里斯琴，你能感觉得到她吗？她是那么的活泼！”

自从你在威尼斯见了你家里的一个朋友之后，你就想为我们的女儿取名为伊拉里娅，因为你发现这个名字在拉丁语里的意思是“永远快乐”。

在伊拉里娅出生前我们就见过她。我们做了3D扫描，通过它我们能看到宝宝的脸盘——她很漂亮。

现在，我是如此感激我们曾用扫描仪看过我们的女儿。当预产期错过两周后，离博尔顿家很近的医院决定对你实施引产。我简直无法想象接下来要发生的事情。

伊拉里娅准备要出来时，助产士让你使劲用力，可伊拉里娅的心跳在减速——她处在危险中。

医生们围在我们身边想方设法取出伊拉里娅时，你用恐慌的眼神看着我。终于，她被取出来了，可是她浑身青紫。护士赶紧把她送到婴儿特别护理病房。这时，你尖叫着说：“她还好吗？”可我只能说：“是的，她很

care baby unit. You screamed, "Is she OK?" and all I could say was, "Yes, she's beautiful, just like you."

It breaks my heart you never even saw your daughter, let alone held her. Then your heart rate started going up and your blood pressure started going down. Doctors said they had to get you into theatre straight away.

As they wheeled you out I grabbed your foot and said "I love you". It was the last time I saw you alive.

Minutes later a doctor took me aside and told me Ilaria was showing signs of major brain damage and they didn't expect her to live. I didn't know which of you to turn to first.

I went to see Ilaria in her incubator. Half an hour later doctors told me the news that would change my life forever. There had been massive bleeding and as they tried to operate you'd had a cardiac arrest.

My world fell apart. I remember shouting, "Why?"

You were just 27, healthy as can be, and now you were gone. An aneurysm had caused the bleeding.

No one could have foreseen it; the doctors did all they could. In the chapel of rest you looked like you were sleeping peacefully. I kissed your face and stroked your hair as I sobbed.

I felt totally lost. Then a nurse came to find me and said something amazing had happened and led me to Ilaria. She'd pulled all the tubes out of her chest and nose and was breathing on her own. The nurses said it was a miracle.

It seemed our Ilaria was determined to stay alive. A nurse laid her in my arms and she began to cry. "Don't worry, Daddy's here," I told her, and she immediately stopped crying.

漂亮，就像你一样。”

你从来没有亲眼见到我们的女儿，更别说抱一抱她了，这让我无比心碎。接着你的心率开始升高，你的血压开始降低。医生说要把你直接转移到手术室。

当你被他们推走的时候，我抓住你的腿说："我爱你。"那就是我最后一次见你了。

几分钟过后，一位医生把我拉到旁边跟我说，伊拉里娅的大脑有受到损伤的迹象，他们没有指望她能活下来。我不知道，你和女儿之间，我该先照顾谁。

我去看了躺在恒温箱里的伊拉里娅。半小时后，医生告诉我一个足以永远改变我命运的消息：当他们给你注射了强心剂后，想要为你做手术的时候，你大出血。

我的世界天崩地裂了，记得那时我大叫："为什么？"

你才 27 岁啊，曾经的你是那么的健康，如今你却就这样走了。动脉瘤导致了大出血。

没有人能够预料到，医生也尽力了。在医院的小礼堂里，你看上去好像只是静静地睡着了。我亲吻着你的脸颊，抚摸着你的头发，泪水浸湿了你的脸颊和头发。

我完全丧失了自我。这时，来了一个护士，她跟我说奇迹出现了，她带我去看伊拉里娅。他们已经把她胸腔里、鼻子里的导管取出来了，她正自由地呼吸着。护士们都说这是一个奇迹。

看样子我们的伊拉里娅决定要坚强地活着了。一个护士把她放在我的手上，她立刻大哭起来 。"别哭，爸爸在这儿呢！"我这样对她说，她立刻就停止了哭泣。

我们的女儿活下来了。

Our daughter was going to live.

It was as if you'd said, "God, you can have me, but you're not having my daughter."

Suddenly, from feeling I had nothing left to live for, I had Ilaria. I changed her first nappy, gave her first bottle—I thought about how you'd have done it and tried to do it the same way.

But then it was back to the terrible reality—your funeral.

Four hundred people attended as the vicar who'd married us buried you just three years later.

And then, two days later I brought Ilaria home from the hospital.

That first night I lay in our bed, Ilaria beside me in her cot and I talked to you. "Jo, you should be here, I need you," I said. I so desperately wished you were lying beside me.

I spent my days in tears. At night I'd lay Ilaria next to me and tell her about you—how, beautiful, good and kind you were.

Photos of you were all over the house and I'd hold Ilaria close to them so she could see you.

And as she gets older, I do other things to bring you into her life. I try to cook things I know you'd have made to make our beautiful Ilaria know her mum, even if she doesn't remember you.

I hope you can hear me when I say: "I miss you Joanne but thank you for our wonderful daughter." I just wish you were here to enjoy her.

When Ilaria was a year old she was diagnosed with cerebral palsy which means she is unlikely to walk. She'll never speak properly and will require constant care. That's when I pulled myself together. I needed to, to give Ilaria the

就好像是你跟上帝说："上帝啊，你可以带走我，但请别带走我的女儿。"

突然间，我从不知道为什么而活着的情绪里走了出来，因为我有了伊拉里娅。我为她换下第一块尿布，我给她第一个奶瓶——我总会想着你是怎么做的，然后用同样的方式做这些事。

但是，我仍旧逃脱不了残酷的现实——你的葬礼。

400 人参加了你的葬礼。时隔三年，曾经为我们主持婚礼的牧师现在正主持着你的葬礼。

两天后，我把伊拉里娅从医院抱回了家。

第一天晚上，我躺在我们的床上，伊拉里娅就在我的身旁，她睡在自己的婴儿床上，而我在和你聊天。"乔，你应该在这里的，我需要你。"我说着，我是如此希望你能躺在我的身旁。

我终日以泪洗面。晚上的时候，我把伊拉里娅放在我的身旁，告诉她关于你的事——告诉她你是一个美丽、善良、贤惠的人。

房间里到处都是你的照片。我抱着她凑近这些照片，好让她能看见你。

随着她慢慢地长大，我又做了其他的事情，为的是把你带进她的生活。我试着做一些我知道你会为她做的食物给伊拉里娅，让我们的漂亮女儿知道她的妈妈，就算她不记得你。

我希望你能听到我说："我想你，乔安娜，谢谢你给我一个这么漂亮的女儿。"我只希望你能在我身旁与我分享她的一切。

伊拉里娅一岁的时候，她被诊断患有大脑麻痹症，这意味着她不能走路，她也无法正常地说话，而且一直需要别人的照顾。就是从那时起，我振作起来，因为我要给伊拉里娅最好的生活。

生活虽然很艰苦，可也很美好。我们俩就像是两个小伙伴一样。现在，她快四岁了，长得几乎跟你一模一样。

best life I can.

Although it's hard it's wonderful too, we're like two little mates. She's nearly four now and looks just like you.

And what a personality. Although she can only say a few words—"Hiya!" is her favorite—she gives me so much love and affection. She's a real cheeky little thing, and can wrap me right round her little finger.

I gave up my job as an area sales manager so that I could devote my time to Ilaria. Every morning she attends Rainbow House, where they specialize in helping children like her.

Every time I look at her I get comfort because she's a living part of you Joanne, your legacy.

I just want you to know that whatever happens I will bring up Ilaria in a way you would have been proud of—and she will always know how special her mummy was.

I love you my darling,

Christian

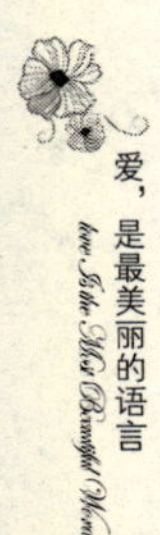

多可爱的小人儿啊！虽然她只能说一些单词——“你好！”是她最爱说的了——可她给了我许多爱和欢喜。她真的是个十足厚脸皮的小家伙，她能用她的小手指把我抓个正着。

我辞去了地区销售经理的工作，这样我才能把全部的时间投在伊拉里娅身上。她每天早上都会去彩虹之家，那里专门帮助像她一样的小孩。

每一次看到她的时候，我都深感安慰，因为她是你——乔安娜生命的延续，是你留给我的宝贵遗产。

我只是想让你知道，无论发生什么事情，我都会用一种让你骄傲的方式把伊拉里娅抚养长大——她永远都会记住她的妈妈是多么的特别。

我爱你，亲爱的。

克里斯琴

Never Say Goodbye

为爱不分手

◎ Crystal Kanone

If I could take this moment forever,
Turn the pages of my mind
To another place and time,
We would never say goodbye.

If I could find the words, I would speak them,
Then I wouldn't be tongue-tied,
When I looked into your eyes,
We would never say goodbye.

If I could stop the moon ever rising,
Day would not become the night,
I wouldn't feel this cold inside,
And we would never say goodbye.

I wish that our dreams were frozen,

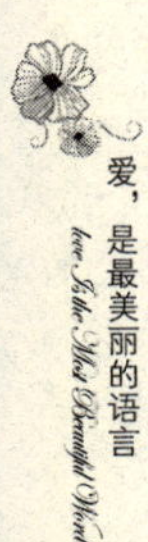

如果我可以永远拥有这一刻，
将我心中的记忆
带回到另一个时间和地点，
我们永远不会说再见。

如果我可以找到这些话，我一定把它们说出来，
这样我的舌头就不会打结，
当我注视着你的眼睛，
我们永远不会说再见。

如果我可以永远地阻止月亮升起来，
白天就不会变成黑夜，
我就不会感到内心的寒冷，
我们也永远不会说再见。

我希望我们的梦可以冻结，

Then our hearts would not be broken,

When we let each other go...

If I could steal this moment forever,

Paint a picture—perfect smile,

So our story stayed alive,

We would never say goodbye.

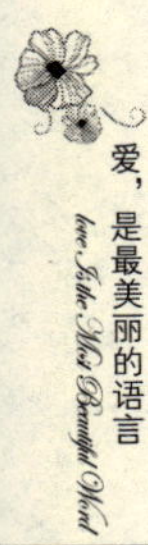

那么我们的心也就不会破碎，

当我们放开彼此的手时……

如果我可以永远的偷走这一刻，

画一幅图画——完美的微笑，

那么我们的故事将会继续上演，

我们永远不会说再见。

Chapter 3 爱是最美的语言

At first it was hard to say, "I love you." But my eyes, my hands, and my heart kept saying it for me... until "I love you" became the most beautiful words of all our moments together.

一开始时，很难开口说“我爱你”。可是我的眼睛、我的双手和我的心，都一直在诉说着……直到“我爱你”成为我们共度时光时最动听的语言。

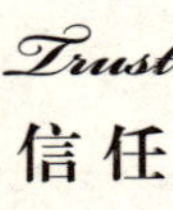

信任

◎ Rita Phil

I remember the date and what you wore and what the weather was like on the day we first liked each other. I also remember that you said hello in a voice that sounded like love.

At first it was hard to say, “I love you.” But my eyes, my hands, and my heart kept saying it for me... until “I love you” became the most beautiful words of all our moments together. I didn’t know that love could be this way.

I didn’t know that love could be my food and drink... my sun all day, my dreams at night, my thoughts, words, fears, hopes and joy! I have a treasure in my heart... a priceless collection of memories that remind me of your love.

I remember one day when everything went wrong. It was one of those days until you met me after school, turning my day happy with your smile. I love you, **encircling**[①] my happiness with your arms. I love the **childlike**[②] you, when you say things in that cute little voice. I love the tender you, holding my hand gently as we walk in the shadows of the street.

---

① encircling [in'sə:kl] vt. 环绕，包围；绕行

② childlike [tʃaildlaik] adj. 天真的；单纯的；坦率的；孩子般的

美丽语录

Time would take away many memories, but it can't take away my mood to love you.

时间会带走很多回忆，但它带不走我决意爱你的心情。

我还记得我们第一次约会、那天的天气和你身上穿的衣服，因为我们从那天开始喜欢上了彼此。我也记得，你跟我打招呼的声音中充满了爱意。

一开始时，很难开口说“我爱你”。可是我的眼睛、我的双手和我的心，都一直在诉说着……直到“我爱你”成为我们共度时光时最动听的语言。我以前从来不知道爱情也可以这样。

我一直不知道爱情可以成为我的食物和饮品……可以成为一天中的太阳，可以成为黑夜里的美梦，可以成为我的思想、言语、担忧、希望和喜悦！一份无价的回忆成了我心中的宝藏，它让我不断回想起你的爱。

我还记得那一天，所有的事情都变得反常了。从那天起，每天放学后你再也不来见我了，你再也不会用微笑开启我幸福的一天了。我爱曾经那个用双臂围绕着我的幸福的你。我爱曾经那个会用孩子气的声音和我说话的幼稚的你。我爱曾经那个轻轻挽着我的手漫步在林荫小道上的温柔的你。

Four weeks ago when coming home from school, I saw someone from the back and thought it was you. I ran to her, calling your name... and when she turned, seeing my surprise and disappointment, she looked disappointed too, knowing she wasn't the one, knowing that her face wasn't the one who brought me such joy.

Do I trust you? What a silly question. Of course I trust you. I trust you completely (almost)! But without the almost I probably wouldn't love you in the first place. If you should go away, years will begin to fade away the memories.

My heart and skin will still remember the way it felt to be close to you. And my hands would still remember the way it felt to hold you in my arms and clearly feel the touch of you. I'm glad that we're like singing birds, free to fly away in search of other songs and eager, always eager to return.

I love you, Roxana, and I trust you more than I trust myself and remember this: you and I will always be "one" as long as I live and that's a promise.

四个星期以前，在放学回家的路上，我看到一个背影很像你的人，我边叫着你的名字边朝她跑去，我原以为那就是你。可是，当她转过头看到我那惊讶而失望的表情时，她也露出了失望的表情，因为她知道自己不是我要找的、能给我带来快乐的那个人。

我可以信任你吗？这是一个多么愚蠢的问题。当然，我信任你，我完全信任你（几乎）！可是，如果没有了这种“几乎”，我就不会对你一见钟情。如果你要离我而去，几年后你就会慢慢将那些记忆遗忘。

我的心和肌肤还记得靠近你时的感觉，我的双手还记得拥抱你时的感觉，也清楚地记得抚摸你时的感觉。我很庆幸我们就像是唱歌的小鸟，可以自由飞翔着去寻找其他的歌曲，而后又很急切地想要回到原点。

我爱你，罗克珊娜，我对你的信任已经超过了对自己的信任。请你记住：只要我活着，我将和你永远融为一体，这便是我许下的承诺。

The Road to Happiness

幸福之道

© Bertrand Russell

It is a commonplace among moralists that you cannot get happiness by pursuing it. This is only true if you pursue it unwisely. Gamblers at Monte Carlo are pursuing money, and most of them lose it instead, but there are other ways of pursuing money, which often succeed. So it is with happiness. If you pursue it by means of drink, you are forgetting the hang-over. Epicurus pursued it by living only in congenial society and eating only dry bread, supplemented by a little cheese on feast days. His method proved successful in his case, but he was a **valetudinarian**①, and most people would need something more vigorous. For most people, the pursuit of happiness, unless supplemented in various ways, is too abstract and theoretical to be adequate as a personal rule of life. But I think that whatever personal rule of life you may choose it should not, except in rare and heroic cases, be incompatible with happiness.

There are a great many people who have all the material conditions of happiness, i.e. health and a sufficient income, and who, nevertheless, are profoundly unhappy. In such cases it would seem as if the fault must lie with a

① valetudinarian ['væi,tju:di'nεəriən] n. 体弱多病的人；过分担心自己健康的人

美丽语录

Remember that happiness is a way of travel, not a destination.

记住幸福是行进中的旅程，而不是目的地。

道德家们常说：幸福是不可追求的。其实，只有用不明智的方式追求才会这样。蒙特卡洛城的赌徒们追求的是金钱，但多数人却把钱都输光了；而另外一些追求金钱的方法却常常能够成功。追求幸福也是如此。如果你通过豪饮来追求幸福，那你便忘记了醉酒之后的不适。埃毕丘鲁斯追求幸福的方法就是和意气相投的人住在一起，只吃不涂黄油的面包，只在节日时才涂上一点奶酪。对他来说，他的方法是成功的。可不幸的是，他体弱多病，而大多数人需要的是精力充沛。对大多数人来说，除非你有别的补充方法，否则这种追求幸福的方式太过抽象和脱离实际，不太适合作为个人的生活准则。不过，在我看来，无论你选择何种生活准则，除了一些少数的英雄人物的例子，都必须和幸福相容。

很多人拥有获得幸福的所有条件，如健康的体魄和充足的收入，可他们却非常不快乐。这种情况下，似乎是生活的理论出错了。从某种意义上来讲，我们可以说所有关于生活的理论都是错误的。我们总以为我们和动

wrong theory as to how to live. In one sense, we may say that any theory as to how to live is wrong. We imagine ourselves more different from the animals than we are. Animals live on impulse, and are happy as long as external conditions are favorable. If you have a cat it will enjoy life if it has food and warmth and opportunities for an occasional night on the tiles. Your needs are more complex than those of your cat, but they still have their basis in instinct. In civilized societies, especially in English-speaking societies, this is too apt to be forgotten. People propose to themselves some one paramount objective, and restrain all impulses that do not minister to it. A businessman may be so anxious to grow rich that to this end he sacrifices health and private affections. When at last he has become rich, no pleasure remains to him except harrying other people by **exhortations**① to imitate his noble example. Many rich ladies, although nature has not endowed them with any spontaneous pleasure in literature or art, decide to be thought cultured, and spend boring hours learning the right thing to say about fashionable new books that are written to give delight, not to afford opportunities for dusty snobbism.

If you look around at the men and women whom you can call happy, you will see that they all have certain things in common. The most important of these things is an activity which at most gradually builds up something that you are glad to see coming into existence. Women who take an instinctive pleasure in their children can get this kind of satisfaction out of bringing up a family. Artists and authors and men of science get happiness in this way if their own work seems good to them. But there are many humbler forms of the same kind of pleasure. Many men who spend their working life in the city devote their

① exhortation [ˌegzɔːˈteiʃən] n. 规劝；告诫

物之间的区别很大。动物仰仗冲动而活，只要客观条件有利，它们就会快乐。如果你养了一只猫，它只要有东西可吃，感觉到温暖，偶尔还能在晚上的时候去寻欢，它就会很快乐。你的需求比猫的要来得复杂些，但它们仍然是以本能为基础的。在文明社会中，特别是在讲英语的国家，这一点很容易被遗忘。人们为自己制定了一个最高目标，尽力克制不利于实现这个目标的所有冲动。商人可能因为想要发财而最终失去了健康和爱情。当他最终成为富翁时，除了苦心劝导别人效仿自己而让别人感到心烦，他并没有得到快乐。那些有钱的贵妇，即便她们天生没有欣赏文学和艺术的细胞，她们也执意要让别人觉得自己很有教养，花费了大量的时间学习如何谈论流行的新书。这些书是为了给人以快乐而写的，而不是为人们提供一个附庸风雅的机会。

如果你仔细观察身边那些你认为是幸福的男女们，你会发现他们身上有着某些共同点，其中最重要的一点就是：追求幸福本身。在大多数情况下它本身就是一个很有趣的活动，并能逐渐地让你的愿望得以实现。生性喜欢孩子的妇女可以从养育孩子的过程中得到满足。艺术家、作家和科学家如果对自己的工作感到满意，他们也可以用同样的方式获得幸福。不过，也有一些较低层次的快乐。许多在大城市里工作的人们，周末时也愿意在自家花园里进行一些无偿的劳作，等到春天时，他们就可以尽情享受自己

weekends to voluntary and unremunerated toil in their gardens, and when the spring comes, they experience all the joys of having created beauty.

The whole subject of happiness has, in my opinion, been treated too solemnly. It had been thought that man cannot be happy without a theory of life or a religion. Perhaps those who have been rendered unhappy by a bad theory may need a better theory to help them to recovery, just as you may need a tonic when you have been ill. But when things are normal a man should be healthy without a tonic and happy without a theory. It is the simple things that really matter. If a man delights in his wife and children, has success in work, and finds pleasure in the alternation of day and night, spring and autumn, he will be happy whatever his philosophy may be. If, on the other hand, he finds his wife fateful, his children's noise unendurable, and the office a nightmare; if in the daytime he longs for night, and at night sighs for the light of day, then what he needs is not a new philosophy but a new regimen—a different diet, or more exercise, or what not.

Man is an animal, and his happiness depends on his physiology more than he likes to think. This is a humble conclusion, but I cannot make myself disbelieve it. Unhappy businessmen, I am convinced, would increase their happiness more by walking six miles every day than by any conceivable change of philosophy.

亲自创造的美景带来的快乐。

在我看来，关于幸福的整个话题都被过于严肃地对待了。过去人们一直觉得，没有生活理论和宗教信仰的人是不会幸福的。也许那些因为生活理论不好而导致不快乐的人需要一种较好的理论让他们重新快乐起来，就像你生病之后需要补药来帮助恢复一样。但是，正常情况下，一个人不吃补药也应当是健康的，没有理论也应当是幸福的。真正起作用的是一些简单的事情。如果一个男人喜爱他的妻儿，事业有成，而且不论白天黑夜，春去秋来，总是很快活。那么，不管他的生活理论是什么，他都是幸福的。相反，如果他讨厌自己的妻子，忍受不了孩子的吵闹，并且讨厌上班；如果他白天时盼望夜晚，而到了晚上又渴望天明，那么他需要的就不是理论，而是一种新的生活——改变饮食习惯，多锻炼自己等等。

人类也是动物，他的幸福更多时候取决于他的生理状况而非思想状况。虽然这是一个庸俗的结论，但我却深信不疑。我相信，不幸福的商人与其寻找其他理论让自己幸福，倒不如每天步行六公里，也许后者会更有效。

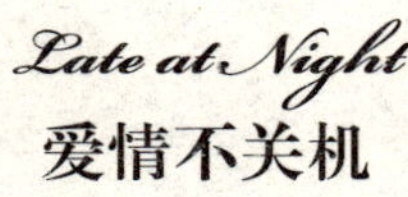

爱情不关机

◎ Anonywous

Today, my friend asked me a question. At night, do you **turn off**[①] your cell phone? If you don't, whom do you leave it on for?

I usually do not turn off my cell phone. Why? I have no idea. After reading an article, I seemed to understand a little bit: for that little bit of caring. I am now sharing this story with you.

The girl would turn her cell phone off and put it by her photo on the desk every night before going to bed. This habit had been with her ever since she bought the phone.

The girl had a very close boyfriend. When they couldn't meet, they would either call or send messages to each other. They both liked this type of communication.

One night, the boy really missed the girl. When he called her, however, the girl's cell phone was off because she was already asleep. The next day, the boy asked the girl to leave her cell phone on at night because when he needed to find her and could not, he would be worried.

① turn off 关掉

美丽语录

A person, be good to yourself; Two person, treat each other.

一个人时，善待自己；两个人时，善待对方。

朋友今天问了我一个问题。深夜，你的手机会关机吗？如果不关，那是为谁而开呢？

我通常都不关机。为什么？我不清楚。但读完这篇文章后，我似乎有所了解：只为那一丝牵挂。现在，就让我与你一起分享这个故事。

每晚睡觉前，女孩都会关掉手机，放在桌上的照片旁。从她买手机起，就一直保持着这个习惯。

女孩有个亲密的男朋友。不见面时，他们会打电话或发信息给对方。他们都喜欢这种交流方式。

一天晚上，男孩很挂念女孩。但他给她打电话时，女孩关机了，因为她已经睡着了。次日，男孩对女孩说，希望她晚上不要关机，因为他想找她时，却找不到，他会很担心。

From that day forth, the girl began a new habit. Her cell phone never shut down at night. Because she was afraid that she might not be able to hear the phone ring in her sleep, she tried to stay very **alert**[①]. As days passed, she became thinner and thinner. Slowly, a gap began to form between them.

The girl wanted to **revive**[②] their relationship. One night, she called the boy. However, what she got was a sweet female voice, "Sorry, the subscriber you dialed is power off."

The girl knew that her love had just been turned off.

After a long time, the girl had a new love. No matter how well they got along, the girl, however, refused to get married. In the girl's heart, she always remembered that boy's words and the night when that phone was power off.

The girl still kept the habit of leaving her cell phone on all throughout the night, but not expecting that it would ring.

One night, the girl caught ill. In a moment of fluster, instead of calling her parents, she dialed the new boyfriend's cell phone. The boy was already asleep but his cell phone was still on.

Later, the girl asked the boy, "Why don't you turn your cell phone off at night?"

The boy answered, "I'm afraid that if you need anything at night and aren't able to find me, you'll worry."

The girl finally married the boy.

Late at night, do you turn off your cell phone?

---

① alert [ə'lə:t] adj. 警觉的；留神的；机敏的
② revive [ri'vaiv] v. 苏醒，复苏；恢复精力

从那天起，女孩开始了新的习惯，晚上不关手机。因为她害怕他打来电话，而自己睡觉又听不到，于是女孩经常保持警惕。日子一天天过去了，她也日渐消瘦。渐渐地，他们之间出现了隔阂。

女孩想要维系他们的关系。一天晚上，她给男孩打电话，却听到了一个甜美的女声："对不起，您所拨打的电话已关机。"

女孩明白了，她的爱也关机了。

很久以后，女孩有了新的爱情。但无论他们相处得有多好，女孩还是拒绝结婚。在她心中，还会时常想起那个男孩的话，还有那个关机的夜晚。

女孩仍然保持着整夜开机的习惯，但是不再期待它会响起。

一天晚上，女孩生病了。慌乱中，本想给父母打电话，却打到了新男友那里。男孩已经睡了，但手机依旧开着。

后来，女孩问男孩："为什么整晚开着手机？"

男孩回答说："我担心你晚上有需要时找不到我，会着急。"

最终，女孩嫁给了这个男孩。

深夜，你的手机开着吗？

Distant Admirer

遥望着你的爱慕者

◎ Kevin Carey

Cary is very popular in his college and nearly everybody knows him. He is a basketball star. And for this reason, he has become the pride of the college, envy of the boys, and hero of the girls. Among his many admirers is a girl called Nola.

Nola is Cary's classmate, and Professor Johnson's daughter. Mr. Johnson is a strict father, and in a family where a sports star is not so highly regarded, Nola never dares to mention Gary's name. In the school, they seldom speak to each other and always keep a certain distance.

Nola's family lives on the campus and there is a big sports ground near their house. Every afternoon, after school, Cary would spend at least one hour practicing basketball before returning home. Nola lives on the third floor, and from their **balcony**① she can see the sports ground. As a habit, Nola would sit in a chair on the balcony, reading or doing her homework every day when she comes home. Sometimes she would raise her head to watch Gary shoot or count how many times he can hit the basket.

① balcony ['bælkəni] n. 阳台，露台；包厢

美丽语录

Action may not always bring happiness, but there is no happiness without action.

行动不一定带来幸福，不行动就肯定没幸福。

凯里在大学时是个十分受欢迎的篮球明星，几乎人人都知道他。正是因为如此，他成了学院的骄傲，男同学嫉妒他，女同学则把他当成英雄。有一个名叫诺拉的女孩，是众多仰慕者中的一个。

诺拉是约翰逊教授的女儿，是凯里的同班同学。在家里，约翰逊先生是一个很严厉的父亲，而一个体育明星在这样的家庭是得不到太高评价的。因此，诺拉在家中从未提过凯里的名字。在学校里，两个人几乎很少说话，而且彼此之间总是保持一定的距离。

诺拉的家就在大学校园里，她家附近有一个很大的操场。每天下午放学以后，凯里都会在那里至少练习一个小时的篮球，然后才回家。诺拉的家住在三楼，她从阳台上就能够看到操场。每天放学回家后，诺拉总是习惯坐在阳台的椅子上，读书或者写作业。有时，她会抬起头，看着凯里投篮，或者数他进了多少次球。

Cary doesn't seem to pay any attention to Nola on the balcony.

One afternoon, Nola moved her chair into the room to **avoid**[1] the breeze outside. But she could still hear the noise from the sports ground. The noise suddenly stopped and the sports ground became very quiet. Nola thought it strange and looked through the window.

She saw Cary **bending do wn**[2] there and writing something on the ground with a piece of chalk. What was he writing? She wondered. Cary finished writing and stood up, he picked up his bag and dragged his way home.

After Cary left, Nola went down quickly and walked quietly to the sports ground. When she got to the place where Cary had just stayed, she found these words, "Nola, why didn't you watch me play?"

She picked up the chalk end on the ground and added below the line, "But yes, I did."

① avoid [ə'vɔid] v. 避开；避免

② bend down 深深地弯下腰，深鞠一躬

然而，凯里似乎没有注意到阳台上的诺拉。

一天下午，外面起风了，诺拉就把椅子搬进了房间。但是，她仍然能够听到操场上传来的球声。突然，球声消失了，操场变得非常安静。诺拉觉得有点反常，便透过窗子向外看去。

她看见，凯里蹲在操场上，拿着一支粉笔在地上写着什么。诺拉很好奇，“他在写些什么呢？”写完之后，凯里站起身，背起书包，拖着沉重的步伐回家了。

见凯里离开了，诺拉迅速地跑下楼，悄悄地来到了操场上。当走到凯里刚才待的地方时，她看到地上写着这样的话：“诺拉，你为什么不看我打球呢？”

诺拉拾起地上的粉笔头，在那句话的后面加上了这样一句：“可是，我真的看了呀。”

Love and Time

爱情与时间

◎ Tom Farley

Once upon a time, there was an island where all the feelings lived: Happiness, Sadness, Knowledge and all of the others, including Love. One day, it was announced to the feelings that the island would sink, so all **constructed**[①] boats and left, except for Love.

Love was the only one who stayed. Love wanted to hold out until the last possible moment.

When the island had almost sunk, Love decided to ask for help.

Richness was passing by Love in a grand boat. Love said, "Richness, can you take me with you?" Richness answered, "No, I can't. There is a lot of gold and silver in my boat. There is no place here for you."

Love decided to ask **Vanity**[②] who was also passing by in a beautiful **vessel**[③]. "Vanity, please help me!" "I can't help you, Love. You are all wet and might damage my boat," Vanity answered.

Sadness was closed by, so Love asked, "Sadness, Let me go with you." "Oh...

① construct [kən'strʌkt] v. 建造，构成；创立

② vanity ['væniti] n. 自负；虚荣；无价值

③ vessel ['vesl] n. 船，舰

美丽语录

Don't promise me forever, just love me day by day.

不必承诺永远，只要爱我一天又一天。

很久以前，一个小岛上住着所有的情感：快乐，悲伤，智慧以及其他一切情感，当然还有爱情。有一天，突然有消息声称这座小岛将会沉没，所有的情感都造好了船准备离开，除了爱情。

爱情是唯一一个留下来的，爱情希望能够坚持到最后一刻。

当小岛即将没顶之际，爱情决定寻求帮助。

财富开着一条大船经过。爱情问："财富，你可以带上我吗？"财富答道："不，我不能。我的船上装满了金银财宝，装不下你了。"

爱情决定问开着漂亮的船从旁边经过的虚荣。"虚荣，请你救救我吧！""我帮不了你，爱情，你浑身湿透了，会弄脏我的船的！"

悲伤也在附近，于是爱情问："悲伤，带我一起走吧。""噢……爱情，我是那么痛苦，痛苦得只想一个人呆着！"

Love, I am so sad that I need to be myself!"

Happiness passed by Love, too. But she was so happy that she did not even hear when Love called her.

Suddenly, there was a voice, "Come, Love, I will take you." It was an elder. So blessed and overjoyed, Love even forgot to ask the elder where they were going. When they arrived at dry land, the elder went her own away.

Realizing how much was owed the elder, Love asked Knowledge, another elder, "Who helped me?"

"It was Time," Knowledge answered.

"Time?" asked Love. "But why did Time help me?"

Knowledge smiled with deep wisdom and answered, "Because only Time is capable of understanding how valuable Love is."

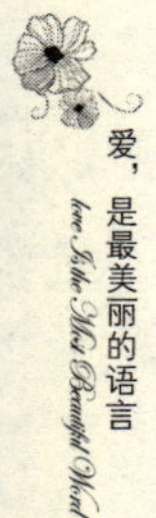

快乐也经过了爱情，可是她快乐过头了，没有听见爱情的呼唤。

突然，一个声音响起，“来吧，爱情，我来帮你。”那是一位长者。爱情十分高兴，甚至忘了问这位长者要去哪儿。当他们抵达陆地时，老人独自离开了。

爱情意识到自己亏欠老人很多，于是问身边的另一个长者智慧，“帮我的那个是谁？”

智慧老人答道：“是时间。”

“时间？可是时间为什么要帮助我？”爱情不解。

智慧意味深长地笑着，答道：“因为只有时间才能理解爱是多么宝贵。”

Russell on Affection
罗素论爱

◎ Russell

The best type of affection is **reciprocally**[①] life-giving; each receives affection with joy and gives it without effort, and each finds the whole world more interesting in consequence of the existence of this reciprocal happiness. There is, however, another kind, by no means uncommon, in which one person sucks the vitality of the other, one receives what the other gives, but gives almost nothing in return.

Some very vital people belong to this bloodsucking type. They extract the vitality from one victim after another, but while they prosper and grow interesting, those upon whom they live grow pale and **dim**[②] and dull. Such people use others as means to their own ends, and never consider them as ends in themselves. **Fundamentally**[③] they are not interested in those whom for the moment they think they love; they are interested only in the stimulus to their own activities, perhaps of a quite impersonal sort.

Evidently this springs from some defect in their nature, but it is one not

① reciprocally [ri'siprəkli] adv. 相互地；互惠地；相反地
② dim [dim] adj. 暗淡的；模糊的；看不清楚的
③ fundamentally [ˌfʌndə'mentli] adv. 基础地；根本地；重要地

美丽语录

Don't promise me forever, just love me day by day.

不必承诺永远，只要爱我一天又一天。

最好的那种爱是能让彼此愉快的爱；彼此很愉快地接受，很自然地给予，并且因为有了这种互利互惠的快乐，彼此都觉得这个世界变得更加有趣。然而，还有一种并不罕见的爱，那就是一方吸收着另一方的活力，接受着另一方的给予，而他这一方却毫无回报。

那些生命力极其旺盛的人就属于这吸血的一类。他们把一个又一个受害者的活力吸尽，然而，当他们越发生机勃勃、兴致盎然的时候，那些受害者却变得越来越苍白、黯淡和迟钝。这些人将他人当成自己实现最终目标的工具，却从不考虑他人也有他自己的目标。他们一时以为自己很爱那些人，但其实他们根本就对那些人不感兴趣；他们感兴趣的是给自己的活动添加的刺激，而他们的活动可能也是属于毫无人情味可言的。

显然，这种情况源于他们本性上的某种缺陷，但这种缺陷不容易诊断

altogether easy either to diagnose or to cure. It is a characteristic frequently associated with great ambition, and is rooted, I should say, in an unduly one-sided view of what makes human happiness. Affection in the sense of a genuine reciprocal interest of two persons in each other, not solely as means to each other's good, but rather as a combination having a common good, is one of the most important elements of real happiness, and the man whose ego is so enclosed within steel walls that this enlargement of it is impossible misses the best that life has to offer, however successful he may be in his career. A too powerful ego is a prison from which a man must escape if he is to enjoy the world to the full. A capacity for genuine affection is one of the marks of the man who has escaped from this prison of self. To receive affection is by no means enough; affection which is received should liberate the affection which is to be given, and only where both exist in equal measure does affection achieve its best possibilities.

From Russell's Views on Life

或者治愈。它往往和野心有关，我必须说，同时也是由于总是不恰当地从单方面考虑世间幸福的缘故。两个人相互关心意义上的爱，不仅是促进彼此幸福的手段，还是促进共同幸福的手段，是影响真正幸福的最重要因素之一。凡是把自己禁锢起来的人，无论他在事业上取得了多大的成功，他都必将错失人生中最好的东西。太强的自我就如一座监狱，如果你想充分地享受人生，那就必须先从那座监狱中逃脱。仅仅接受爱是远远不够的；接受的爱应该是能激发你也献出自己的爱，只有接受的爱和释放的爱等量存在时，爱才能达到它的最佳状态。

选自《罗素论人生》

Whatever Love Means—Diana
爱就是一切——黛安娜

◎ Freya Berry

Although neither nor they remembered the occasion, Diana first met her future husband when she was just a baby. It happened during the winter of 1961, when twelve-year-old Charles, Prince of Wales, was visiting his mother's Sandringham retreat.

At the time, your Prince Charles barely glanced at the tiny baby sleeping in her cot. After all, how could a twelve-year-old boy be interested in babies?

But the Prince would eventually take a very keen interest in this particular baby—it would just take some time.

In fact, it would be sixteen years before Prince Charles and Lady Diana Spencer took place in the middle of a farmer's field during a shooting party in November 1977.

It was a cold, rainy, bleak afternoon when sixteen-year-old Diana, dressed in a borrowed parka that was too large for her, boots, and blue jeans, crossed the field to meet the heir to the British **throne**①.

It was almost twilight when the two came face to face near No-bottle

① throne [θrəun] n. 御座，宝座；王权；君王

美丽语录

The greatest happiness in life is that you find the one you love is loving you as well.

人生最大的幸福，是发现自己爱的人正好也爱着自己。

虽然两个人都已记不清那段往事，戴安娜第一次见到她未来的丈夫时，她还只是个孩子。那是在 1961 年的冬天，当时年仅 12 岁的威尔士王储查尔斯正呆在夏丁汉他母亲的休养院。

那时，查尔斯王子根本看都没看那个睡在小床里的小不点。毕竟，12 岁的小男孩怎么会对一个婴儿感兴趣呢?

然而，王子还是对这个婴儿产生了浓厚的兴趣——不过那都是后来的事情了。

实际上，查尔斯王子和戴安娜·斯宾塞女士再次相遇已是 16 年后了。那次相遇是在 1977 年的一次乡村狩猎会上。

那是一个寒风刺骨、阴雨绵绵的下午，16 岁的戴安娜穿着一件借来的过大的毛皮风雪衣，足膝长靴，一条蓝色牛仔裤。她正经过一片狩猎场朝这位英国王位继承人走来。

快到傍晚时，两人才在诺布托树林附近迎面相遇。

Woods.

"What a sad man," Diana thought when she first saw him. The future Princess was intrigued to finally meet the most eligible[①] bachelor in England, though she was not impressed with his five-foot-ten-inch height, thinking to herself that she would tower over him in high heels. But Diana would later say that she admired his beautiful blue eyes.

The Prince later remarked that he thought Diana was "a very jolly and attractive" girl, "full of fun," though Diana herself believed that "he barely noticed me at all."

Diana, it was discovered later, first came to the attention of the royal family when she acted as a bridesmaid[②] for her sister Jane's wedding that April. It was the first major social occasion that Diana attended as a young woman. And many of the royals were surprised at how beautiful and mature the once gawky girl had become.

Even the Queen Mother Prince Charles's grandmother, noticed Diana's beauty, grace, and charm. She complimented the Earl on the fine job he had done in bringing Diana up.

A short time later, Prince Charles sent his valet to hand-deliver a formal invitation for Diana to accompany him that very evening to the opera and a late night dinner at the palace.

Though she was flustered, and the invitation came at such short notice, Diana accepted. She and her roommate, Carolyn Bartholomew, hurried to dress and prepare Diana for her big date. The evening was a success, and an invitation

① eligible ['elidʒəbl] adj. 有资格当选的；法律上合格的；(婚姻等)合适的

② bridesmaid ['braidzmeid] n. 女傧相

当戴安娜第一看见王子时她心里想："多么忧郁的一个人啊！"尽管戴安娜对于他五英尺十英寸的身高并不以为然，心想如果自己穿上高跟鞋肯定会高过他。但这位未来的英国王妃还是很期盼与英国最令人中意的单身汉见面。不过戴安娜后来说她很羡慕他的那双漂亮的蓝眼睛。

虽然戴安娜自认为"他根本没注意过我"，可是王子后来说他觉得戴安娜是个"快乐又动人"的姑娘。

后来人们发现，戴安娜真正引起皇室注意是在那年四月份她姐姐简的婚礼上，当时她是伴娘。那是戴安娜成年后参加的第一个大型社交活动。许多皇室成员看到她的时候都惊呆了，原本那个粗笨难看的小女孩，如今出落成了一个成熟美丽的女人。

甚至连查尔斯王子的祖母王后陛下都注意到了戴安娜的美丽、端庄和魅力。她还称赞了伯爵对戴安娜的栽培。

不久之后，查尔斯王子吩咐随从亲自给戴安娜送来了一张正式的请柬，邀请她当晚和王子一同观看话剧以及出席午夜的王宫宴会。

尽管戴安娜感到局促不安，那张请柬来得太突然，戴安娜还是接受了邀请。她和室友卡洛琳·巴赛洛缪匆匆忙忙地梳洗打扮了一番，并为戴安娜做好了出席这个重大约会的准备。那天晚上玩得非常尽兴。不久，邀请她参加皇室游艇聚会的请柬又接踵而至……

to party on the royal yacht came soon after...

Although she was intimidated by the crown at Balmoral, Diana was wise enough not to stay in the castle itself. She asked for, and was granted, an invitation to stay with her sister Jane and her young husband at their cottage on the Balmoral estate.

The Prince visited Diana there every day, offering to escort her to a barbecue, or extending an invitation for a long walk in the woods.

When Charles went to Switzerland for a ski vacation, Diana missed him terribly. He called her after a day or two, and told Diana he had something important to ask her.

He arrived home on February 3, 1981. Three days later, he arranged to see Diana at Windsor Castle. Later that evening, while Prince Charles was showing Diana the nursery, he asked her to marry him.

To his surprise, Diana treated his proposal as a joke, she actually giggled. But soon she could see that Prince Charles was serious. Despite an insistent voice inside her head that told her she would never be Queen, she accepted his proposal.

Diana told Prince Charles over and over that she loved him.

"Whatever love means." was his reply.

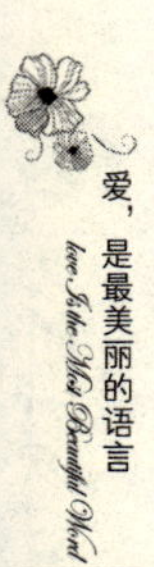

虽然戴安娜对拜尔马洛众王族感到害怕，但她十分明智没有选择住在城堡里。她提出请求，并得到准许，她受到邀请住在姐姐简和简的年轻丈夫在拜尔马洛的别墅中。

王子每天都会去那里拜访她，不是邀请她参加户外烤肉，就是邀请她到树林中进行长时间的散步。

当查尔斯去瑞士滑雪旅行时，戴安娜发了疯地思念他。一两天后查尔斯王子打电话给她，并告诉戴安娜他回英国后，有一些很重要的问题要问她。

1981 年 2 月 3 号，他回来了。三天后，他安排在温莎堡见戴安娜。那天晚上，当查尔斯王子带着戴安娜参观育婴室的时候，他问戴安娜是否愿意嫁给他。

让他惊讶的是，戴安娜把他的求婚当成了一个玩笑，她还咯咯地笑了起来。可不久之后，她就发现查尔斯王子是认真的。尽管她的脑海中不断有个声音在劝诫自己不要想着当王妃，可她还是接受了王子的求婚。

戴安娜一遍又一遍地对王子说她爱他。

“爱就是一切。”他回答道。

趣味课堂

The Meaning of Love
爱的意义·字母篇

A—Accept（接受）接受一切，包括对方的优点和缺点。

B—Belief（信任）互相猜忌的爱情只有分手的结局。

C—Care（关心）关心的程度体现了对对方的重视程度。

D—Digest（理解）对方情绪起伏时，何不用一颗理解的心去安慰他（她）呢?

E—Enjoy（欣赏）欣赏这段爱情带给你的开心和幸福。

F—Freedom（自由）给予对方自由及保密的权利。

G—Give（付出）甘愿付出的爱才是真正的爱。

H—Heart（心）没有心，何以真心相爱?

I—Independence（独立）不要过于依赖对方，成为对方的沉重包袱。

J—Jealousy（妒忌）适当的妒忌和吃醋正好表现了你对对方的重视。

K—Kiss（吻）一吻胜过千言万语，请不要吝啬你的红唇。

L—Love（爱）爱情爱情，没爱哪来情?有空不妨说说“我爱你”，保证比任何礼物还来得开心。

M—Mature（成熟）人成熟一点，爱情自然也会早些成熟。

N—Nature（自然）流于自然的爱情才是细水长流的！

O—Observe（观察）细心观察爱侣的喜好，并适时给予惊喜，比礼物还管用。

P—Protect（保护）无论男朋友女朋友，都要保护另一半免受中伤和侮辱。

Q—Quarter（宽大）对爱侣的错误，应予以原谅，毕竟他（她）是你的最爱。

R—Receive（接收）以欣赏的态度去接受对方的付出。

S—Share（分享）分享欢喜与哀愁，是作为一个伴侣最基本的责任。

T—Tender（温柔）爱人要温柔地爱，男人女人缺乏温柔都不可爱。

U—Understand（明白）站在对方的立场上，将心比心为对方想想。

V—Veracity（诚实）对爱情要有一百倍的诚实，互相欺骗的爱情怎能天长地久。

W—Wait（等待）与他（她）同步成长，共同走完一段人生路。

X—x（乘法符号——感情与日倍增）将爱每天乘以倍数，爱情将无限大，走也走不掉。

Y—Yearn（想念）“小别胜新婚”，CALL 他（她）：“我很想念你！”

Z—Zest（激情）没有激情的爱情如死水一潭，适当的激情可增添乐趣。

Chapter 4

曾有一个人，爱我如生命

I'd rather hold you for a minute than live the rest of life knowing I never could.

我宁愿牵着你的手，过最后一分钟，也不愿在没有你的世界虚度此生。

Love Is More Thicker Than Forget
爱情比忘却厚

◎ E.E. Cummings

Love is more thicker than forget
More thinner than recall
More seldom than a wave is wet
More frequent than to fail

It is most mad and moonly
And less it shall unbe
Than all the sea which only
Is deeper than the sea

Love is less always than to win
Less never than alive
Less bigger than the least begin
Less littler than forgive

It is most sane and sunly

爱情比忘却厚
比回忆薄
比潮湿的波浪多
比失败少

它最痴最癫最疯狂
但和所有
海洋深处的海洋相比
它却更加长久

爱情总是比胜利少见
比活着多见
不比无法理解大
不比原谅小

它最明朗最清晰

And more it cannot die

Than all the sky which only

Is higher than the sky.

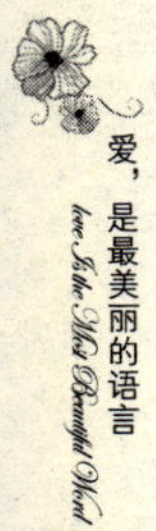

但和所有
比天空更高的天空相比
它却更加不朽

Butterfly Kisses
蝶吻

◎ Ronit Baras

My newlywed husband said the same thing every morning, "You're beautiful today."

One glance in the mirror **revealed**① that it was far from the truth.

A skinny girl with mashed hair on one side of her head and no makeup smiled back at me. I could feel my sticky morning breath.

"Liar," I shot back with a grin.

It was my usual response. My mother's first husband was not a kind man and his **verbal**② and physical abuse forced her and her two children to find a safe place. He showed up on her doorstep one day with roses. She let him in and he beat her with those roses and took advantage of her. Nine months later she gave birth to a 9 lb. 13 oz. baby girl—me.

The harsh words we heard growing up took root. I had trouble seeing myself as someone of value. I had been married two years when I surprised myself. My husband wrapped his arms around me and told me I was beautiful.

---

① reveal [ri'vi:l] v. 展现，揭露；暴露，泄露

② verbal ['və:bəl] adj. 言语的；口头上的；逐字的，照字面的

美丽语录

When I wake up every morning, the greatest joy is gazing upon you and sunshine, that is the future I desire

每天早上醒来，最大的愉悦就是看到你和阳光都在，这就是我想要的未来。

我的新婚丈夫每天早晨都会对我说同样的话："你今天真美！"

我只要往镜子里一瞥就知道他说的根本不是事实。

镜子里有一个瘦瘦的、乱乱的头发倒向一边、没有化妆的女孩，她正微笑地望着我。我还能感觉到早晨起来时嘴里那股难闻的气味。

"撒谎。"我咧嘴笑着答道。

我总是这样回敬我的丈夫。我母亲的第一个丈夫不是一个善良的男人，他粗暴的言语攻击和身体虐待迫使我母亲带着两个孩子去寻找一个安全的地方。有一天，他出现在我母亲的门前，手捧着一束玫瑰花。她让他进了门，他却用那些玫瑰花打了她，还强行占了她的便宜。于是，9 个月后她生下了一个 9 磅 13 盎司重的女孩——就是我。

成长过程中我所听到的那些刺耳的话语深深地埋藏在我心中。我无法将自己看成一个有价值的人。可结婚两年后，我简直惊呆了，因为我的丈

"Thank you," I said.

The same thin girl with the mousy brown hair still stared back at me in the mirror, but somehow the words had finally blossomed in my heart.

A lot of years have passed. My husband has grey in his hair. I'm no longer skinny. Last week I woke up and my husband's face was inches from mine.

"What are you doing?" I asked.

I covered my mouth, trying to hide my morning breath. He reached down and kissed my face.

"What I do every morning," he said.

He leaves in the early hours of the morning while I sleep. I miss our morning conversations, but I had not realized that he continued to tell me that he loved me even while I slept. When he left, I rolled over and hugged my pillow. I envisioned the picture of me lightly snoring with my mouth open and giggled.

What a man! My husband understands my past. He's been beside me as I've grown from an unsure young girl to a confident woman, mother, speaker and author.

But I'm not sure that he understands the part he played in that **transition**①. The words I heard growing up pierced my soul, yet his words pierced even deeper.

This Anniversary Day I plan to wake early. I want to tell Richard how much I love him. He may look in the mirror and see an extra pound or two, or wish for the day when his hair was dark and curly, but all I'll see is the man who saw something in me when I couldn't see it myself, and who leaves butterfly kisses, even after twenty-three years of marriage.

① transition [træn'ziʃən] n. 过渡，过渡期；转变；变革

夫双手拥着我，告诉我我是美丽的。

“谢谢。”我说。

镜子里，同样瘦弱、一头灰褐色头发的女人正盯着我，可那温柔的话语终于让我心花怒放了。

许多年过去了。我的丈夫已经长出了灰白色的头发。我也不再骨瘦如柴。上周的一天早晨，我醒来时发现丈夫的脸离我只有几英寸的距离。

“你在干什么？”我问。

我掩住了自己的嘴，免得让他闻到嘴里的味道。他俯身过来亲吻了我的脸。

“做我每天早晨做的事啊！”他说。

他总是在清晨时就得出门，那时我还在睡觉。我很想念我们之间久违的晨间对话，可我还未意识到他一直在告诉我他爱我，即使在我熟睡的时候。他离开后，我便会转个身，抱着一个枕头。我想象着自己睡觉时打鼾、嘴巴微张的样子，不禁笑出了声。

他就是这样一个男人！我的丈夫知道我的过去。在我从一个不自信的年轻女子变成一个成熟自信的女人、母亲、演讲者、作家的过程中，他一直在我身边。

可我不确定他是否明白在这个转变过程中他所扮演的角色。伴我长大的话语曾那样刺痛我的灵魂，然而，他的话语更是深深地感动了我的灵魂。

今天是结婚周年纪念日，我决定早点起来。我想告诉理查德我有多爱他。照镜子时，他也许会发现自己又发福了，或者期盼着有一天他的头发又是乌黑鬈曲的。可是，在我眼中他是这样一个男人：是他发现了我身上的那些东西，而我却未能发现；即便是在结婚23年后，他还是天天给我留下蝶吻。

Hanover Square
追忆似水年华

◎ Marcel Proust

Can it really be sixty-two years ago that I first saw you?

It is truly a lifetime, I know. But as I gaze into your eyes now, it seems like only yesterday that I first saw you, in that small café in Hanover Square.

From the moment I saw you smile, as you opened the door for that young mother and her newborn baby. I knew. I knew that I wanted to share the rest of my life with you.

I still think of how foolish I must have looked, as I gazed at you, that first time. I remember watching you intently, as you took off your hat and loosely shook your short dark hair with your fingers. I felt myself becoming **immersed**① in your every detail, as you placed your hat on the table and cupped your hands around the hot cup of tea, gently blowing the steam away with your pouted lips.

From that moment, everything seemed to make perfect sense to me. The people in the café and the busy street outside all disappeared into a hazy blur. All I could see was you.

All through my life I have relived that very first day. Many, many times I

① immersed [i'mə:st] adj. 浸入的；受浸礼的；专注的

美丽语录

I enjoy every second of my life because you're in it.

我珍惜生命中的每一秒，因为你在里面。

难道我们的初次相遇，真的发生在62年前吗?

我知道，年华似水，转眼间已是一生。如今，我望着你的眼睛时，当年的初次相遇——就在汉诺广场的那间小咖啡屋里——仿若昨日。

从我见到你迷人微笑的那一刻起，那一刻你正在为一位年轻的母亲和她的小宝宝开门。那一刻我就知道，我想与你共度余生。

现在我还会想起来，第一次我那样盯着你时，样子看起来一定很傻。我就那样目不转睛地看着你，我的目光追随你脱下小黑帽，用手指轻轻拨弄你的黑色短发；追随你把帽子放在桌前，双手举起热气腾腾的茶杯，用你那樱桃小嘴轻轻吹走飘腾的热气。我发觉自己早已被你温柔的举止融化了。

从那一刻起，一切的意义都鲜明了起来。小咖啡屋里的人和屋外繁忙的街道都变得模糊了，我能看到的，只有你。

光阴似箭，可那天的情景却不断地在我的记忆里重演，历历在目。多

have sat and thought about that the first day, and how for a few fleeting moments I am there, feeling again what is like to know true love for the very first time. It pleases me that I can still have those feelings now after all those years, and I know I will always have them to comfort me.

Not even as I shook and trembled uncontrollably in the trenches, did I forget your face. I would sit huddled into the wet mud, terrified, as the hails of bullets and mortars crashed down around me. I would clutch my **rifle**① tightly to my heart, and think again of that very first day we met. I would cry out in fear, as the noise of war beat down around me. But, as I thought of you and saw you smiling back at me, everything around me would be become silent, and I would be with you again for a few precious moments, far from the death and destruction. It would not be until I opened my eyes once again, that I would see and hear the carnage of the war around me.

I cannot tell you how strong my love for you was back then, when I returned to you on leave in the September, feeling battered, bruised and fragile. We held each other so tight I thought we would burst. I asked you to marry me the very same day and I whooped with joy when you looked deep into my eyes and said "yes" to being my bride.

I'm looking at our wedding photo now, the one on our dressing table, next to your jeweler box. I think of how young and innocent we were back then. I remember being on the church steps grinning like a Cheshire cat, when you said how dashing and handsome I looked in my uniform. The photo is old and faded now, but when I look at it, I only see the bright **vibrant**② colors of our youth. I

---

① rifle ['raifl] n. 步枪，来福枪；步枪队

② vibrant ['vaibrənt] adj. 振动的，颤动的；响亮的；活跃的

少次我重新坐下，不断追忆着那天的一切，不断回味着那些稍纵即逝的瞬间，重新体味一见钟情的美丽。消逝的岁月没有把我的爱恋感觉带走，这些感觉会永远陪伴着我，安抚我那短暂的余生。

即使当我在战壕中控制不住地颤抖时，我也不曾忘却你的容颜。我蜷缩在烂泥中，身边是枪林弹雨，硝烟弥漫，我把步枪紧紧地揣在胸前，尽管一颗心惶恐不安，我还是想起了我们初次相遇的那一天。身旁战火呼啸，恐惧让我想要大声呼叫。然而，我想起了你，仿佛看见你在朝我微笑着。这时，周围忽然安静了下来，在这珍贵的瞬间，我觉得自己就在你的身边，远离那些死亡和恐惧。我拼命想要留住这份美好。然而，当我睁开眼时，身旁却依旧是那个血与火的生死战场。

9 月休假回到你身边时，疲惫、脆弱的我没能告诉你在战火纷飞时我对你的爱有多深。我们紧紧地拥抱在一起，仿佛要把对方挤碎。也就在那天，我向你求婚了。当你深深地凝望着我的眼睛，说了“我愿意”时，我欣喜地大喊大叫着。

现在我正看着我们的结婚照片，就是放在梳妆台上的那张，就在你的首饰盒旁。那时的我们是那样的年轻、天真。我还记得，当你说我穿着西装很帅气的时候，站在教堂台阶上的我开心得就像一只露出牙齿嬉笑的猫。

can still remember every detail of the pretty wedding dress your mother made for you, with its fine delicate lace and pretty pearls. If I concentrate hard enough, I can smell the sweetness of your wedding bouquet as you held it so proudly for everyone to see.

I remember being so over enjoyed, when a year later, you gently held my hand to your waist and whispered in my ear that we were going to be a family.

I know both our children love you dearly; they are outside the door now, waiting.

Do you remember how I panicked like a mad man when Jonathon was born? I can still picture you laughing and smiling at me now, as I clumsily held him for the very first time in my arms. I watched as your laughter faded into tears, as I stared at him and cried my own tears of joy.

Sarah and Tom arrived this morning with little Tessie. Can you remember how we both hugged each other tightly when we saw our tiny granddaughter for the first time? I can't believe she will be eight next month. I am trying not to cry, my love, as I tell you how beautiful she looks today in her pretty dress and red shiny shoes, she reminds me so much of you that first day we met. She had her hair cut short now, just like yours was all those years ago. When I met her at the door her smile wrapped around me like a warm glove, just like yours used to do, my darling.

I know you are tired, my dear, and I must let you go. But I love you so much and it hurts to do so.

As we grew old together, I would tease you that you had not changed since we first met. But it is true, my darling. I do not see the wrinkles and grey hair that other people see. When I look at you now, I only see your sweet tender lips

如今，照片已经旧得泛黄了，可当我看见它时，我看到的只是色彩斑斓的青春。至今我还清晰地记得你母亲亲手为你缝制的那件婚纱，那些精致的蕾丝花边和漂亮珍珠配饰。如果我能专心致志地回想，我还能闻到婚礼捧花的甜香。你是那么自豪地捧着那束花，让每个人都能亲眼见证你的幸福。

一年后，你轻轻地把我的手放到你的腹前，并在我的耳边悄悄地告诉我那个让我欣喜若狂的好消息：我们就快有宝宝啦！

我知道我们的孩子都深深地爱着你，他们现在就等候在门外。

你还记得乔纳森出生那天我手足无措的慌张样子吗？当我第一次笨拙地把他抱在怀里时，你正在冲我微笑，至今我还记得你笑话我时的样子。我看着他，我们都不由自主地流下了喜悦的泪水。

今天早晨，撒拉和汤姆带着小缇西也赶到了。你还记得吗？当我们第一次见到这个可爱的小孙女时，我们紧紧地拥抱在一起。简直不敢相信，她下个月就 8 岁了。亲爱的，我正强忍着眼泪告诉你，小家伙今天穿着漂亮的裙子，闪亮的红鞋，她让我立刻想起当年初次相遇时的你。现在，小家伙还剪了个短发，像极了多年前的你。亲爱的，当我在门口看到她的时候，她的笑容就像一幅温暖的手套将我裹住，这竟然也和年轻时的你一样。

亲爱的，我知道你累了，我必须放手让你离开。然而，我有多爱你，就有多心痛。

这些年我们携手一起变老，我总是逗你说，你一点都没变，还和当初第一次见面时一模一样。可这些都是真的，亲爱的。我真的看不到他人眼

and youthful sparkling eyes as we sat and had out first picnic next to that small stream, and chased each other around that big old oak tree. I remember wishing those first few days together would last forever. Do you remember how exciting and wonderful those days were?

I must go now, my darling. Our children are waiting outside. They want to say goodbye to you.

I wipe the tears away from my eyes and bend my frail old legs down to the floor, so that I can kneel beside you. I lean close to you and take hold of your hand and kiss your tender lips for the very last time.

Sleep peacefully, my dear.

I am sad that you had to leave me, but please don't worry. I am content, knowing I will be with you soon. I am too old and too empty now to live much longer without you.

I know it won't be long before we meet again in the small café in Hanover Square.

Goodbye, my darling wife.

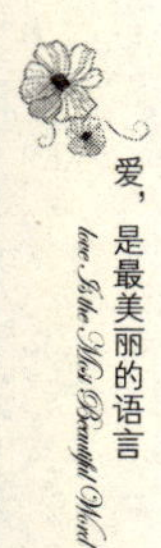

里的皱纹和灰发。现在，当我看着你，我也只能看到红嫩温柔的双唇和年轻有神的眼神，就和我们第一次在小溪边野餐，在巨大的老橡树旁追逐嬉戏时一样。我记得我们曾期盼那些刚开始时一起度过的时光能够永不消逝。你还记得那些日子是多么美好，多么令人激动吗?

亲爱的，我该走了。我们的孩子就在外面等着。他们想要和你说声再见。

我拭去眼角的泪，跪在你的身边，轻轻地靠近你，握住你的双手，最后一次吻你。

亲爱的，安心地睡吧!

分离让我心碎。但是，不要担心，不久之后我们就能重逢，这让我心满意足。如今，我已然老去，世间没有了那个与我生活了一生的你，变得如此的空洞，毫无意义。

我知道，很快，我们就能在汉诺威广场的那间小咖啡屋里重逢。

再见了，我的爱妻。

Every Woman Is Beautiful
每个女人都美丽

◎ Anonymous

A little boy asked his mother "Why are you crying?"

"Because I'm a woman," she told him.

"I don't understand," he said.

His mum just hugged him and said, "And you never will."

Later the little boy asked his father, "Why does mother seem to cry for no reason?"

"All women cry for no reason," was all his dad could say.

The little boy grew up and became a man, still wondering why women cry.

Finally he put in a call to God; and when God got on the phone, he asked, "God, why do women cry so easily?"

God said, "When I made the woman, she had to be special. I made her shoulders strong enough to carry the weight of the world; yet, gentle enough to give comfort."

"I gave her an inner strength to endure childbirth and the **rejection**① that many times comes from her children."

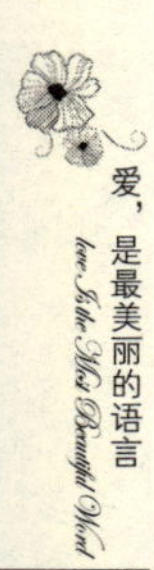
爱，是最美丽的语言
love Is the Most Beautiful Word

① rejection [ri'dʒekʃən] n. 拒绝，退回；摒弃，厌弃；呕出物

美丽语录

Precious things are very few in this world. That is the reason there is just one you.

在这世上珍贵的东西总是罕有，所以这世上只有一个你。

一个男孩问他的妈妈：“你为什么要哭呢？”

妈妈说：“因为我是女人啊。”

男孩说：“我不懂。”

他妈妈抱起他说：“你永远不会懂的。”

后来小男孩就问他爸爸：“妈妈为什么无缘无故地哭呢？”

他爸爸只能说：“所有的女人都会这样。”

小男孩长成了一个男人，但他仍旧不懂女人为什么哭泣。

最后，他打电话给上帝；在上帝拿起电话时，他问道：“上帝，女人为什么那么容易哭泣？”

上帝回答说：“当我创造女人时，就让她很特别。我使她的肩膀坚强得能挑起整个世界；然而，却又柔情似水，能抚慰他人。”

“我让她的内心坚强，能够承受分娩的痛苦，忍受来自孩子的一次次拒

"I gave her a hardness that allows her to keep going when everyone else gives up, and take care of her family through sickness and fatigue[①] without complaining."

"I gave her the sensitivity to love her children under any and all circumstances, even when her child has hurt her very badly."

"I gave her strength to carry her husband through his faults and fashioned her from his rib to protect his heart."

"I gave her wisdom to know that a good husband never hurts his wife, but sometimes tests her strengths and her resolve to stand beside him unfalteringly[②]."

"And finally, I gave her a tear to shed. This is hers exclusively to use whenever it is needed."

"You see, the beauty of a woman is not in the clothes she wears, the figure that she carries, or the way she combs her hair."

"The beauty of a woman must be seen in her eyes, because that is the doorway to her heart, the place where love resides."

Every woman is beautiful.

① fatigue [fə'ti:g] n. 疲劳，劳累；杂役

② unfaltering [ʌn'fɔ:ltəriŋ] adj. 不晃晃摇摇的；坚定的

绝。”

“我赋予她坚韧，使她能在别人放弃的时候继续坚持着，并且无怨无悔地照顾自己的家人渡过疾病与疲劳。”

“我赋予她在任何情况下都会爱孩子的情感，即使她的孩子深深地伤害了她。”

“我赋予她包容她丈夫过错的坚强，并用他的肋骨塑成她来保护他的心。”

“我赋予她智慧，让她知道一个好丈夫是绝不会伤害他的妻子的，但有时我也会考验她支持丈夫的坚持与决心。”

“最后，我让她可以流泪。只要她愿意，这是她所独有的。”

“你看，女人的美丽不是因为她穿的衣服，她保持的体型或者她梳头的方式。”

“女人的美丽必须要从她的眼睛去看，那是她心灵的窗口，是爱居住的地方。”

每个女人都美丽。

If It Comes Back

倘若鸟儿回还

© Charle Eastman

Charles saw them both at the same time: a small white bird and the girl wheeling down the walk. The bird glided downward and rested in the grass; the girl directed the chair smoothly along the sunlit, shadowy walk. She stopped to watch the ducks on the pond and when she shoved the wheels again, Charles stood up. "May I push you?" he called, running across the grass to her. The white bird flew to the top of a tree.

It was mostly he who talked and he seemed afraid to stop for fear she'd ask him to leave her by herself. Nothing in her face had supported the idea of helplessness conveyed by the wheelchair, and he knew that his **assistance**① was not viewed as a favor. He asked the cause of her handicap.

"It was an automobile accident when I was 12," Amy explained.

They went for lunch, and he would have felt **awkward**② except that she knew completely how to take care of herself.

"Do you live with someone?" he asked the next day when they met.

---

① assistance [ə'sistəns] n. 援助，帮助

② awkward ['ɔ:kwəd] adj. 笨拙的；不灵巧的；难操纵的，难对付的

美丽语录

Eternity is not a distance but a decision.

永远不是一种距离，而是一种决定。

查尔斯是在同一时刻看到他们的：一只白色的小鸟和坐着轮椅漫步而来的女孩。小鸟向下滑翔而来，栖息在草丛中；女孩子则缓缓地驾着轮椅，走在阳光照射下婆娑的树影间。她停下来看了看池塘里的鸭子，当她再次用手推动轮椅时，查尔斯一下子站了起来。"我来推你，好吗？"他一面喊着，一面穿过草地朝她跑去。那只小白鸟嗖地一下飞上了树梢。

大多数时间都是他在不停地说话，他似乎担心话一停，她就会请他离开，好让她一个人呆着。她的脸上根本看不到任何因为轮椅而存在的无助表情，因此他知道，自己的帮助并没有被看作是一种恩惠。他问起了导致她残疾的原因。

"我 12 岁那年出了一场车祸。"艾米解释道。

接着，他们一起去吃了午餐。幸好她能完全自理，不然他可就尴尬了。

第二天见面时，他问道："你和什么人住在一起吗？"

"就我自己。"她答道。尽管这正是他所希望得到的答案，但是提出这

"Just myself," she answered. Asking the question made him feel uneasy because of his own loneliness even though he was hoping for this answer.

He came to like to feel the white handles in his grasp, to walk between the two white-rimmed metal wheels. And he grew almost more familiar with the slight wave at the back of her hair than with her eyes or her mouth. Once, he said to the wave at the back of her hair, "I hope I'm the only chair-pusher in your life," but she had only smiled a little and her eyes had admitted nothing.

She cooked dinner for him once in June. He expected her to be proud of her ability to do everything from her seat in the wheelchair—and was faintly disappointed to see that she would not feel pride at what was, for her, simply a matter of course. He watched his own hand pick up the salt shaker and place it on one of the higher unused shelves, and awaited her **plea for**[①] assistance. He didn't know why he'd done it, but the look in her eyes made him realize how cruel his prank was. To make her forget what he'd done, he told her about the little white bird in the park.

"I've seen it, too," she said. "I read a poem once about a little white bird that came to rest on a windowsill and the lady who lived in the house began to put out food for it. Soon the lady fell in love, but it was a mismatched love. Every day the little bird came to the window and the lady put out food. When the love affair was over, the little white bird never returned, but the woman went on putting out the crumbs every day for years and the wind just blew them away."

In July he took her boating frequently. The most awkward event, she felt, was getting in and out of the boat. For Charles, however, these "**freight**[②]

① plea for 恳求，请求
② freight [freit] n.（船运）货物；运费

个问题还是让他有些不安，因为他自己也过得很孤独。

他开始喜欢把轮椅的白色手柄握在手里的感觉，喜欢在那两只镶有白边的金属轮子中间推车行走。他越来越熟悉她那披在身后的、微微起伏的长发，甚至超过了对她的眼睛和嘴唇的熟悉程度。有一次，他对着她波浪一般起伏的长发说："真希望我是你生命中唯一为你推轮椅的人。"但她只是浅浅地一笑，眼里没有任何表示。

6 月的时候，她曾为他做过一顿晚餐。她能坐在轮椅上做任何事情，他以为她会引以为豪——可她仅仅把这当作一件理所当然的事，并无自豪感可言，这让他有些失落。他亲手拿起盐瓶，把它放到一块较高的、不常用的碗柜搁板上，然后等着她请求帮助。他不明白自己为什么要这么做，但她的眼神让他意识到，他的恶作剧有多么残酷。为了让她忘掉自己刚才的愚蠢行为，他跟她说起了公园里的那只小白鸟。

"我也看见过那只小白鸟。"她说，"我曾经读过一首诗，诗中的小白鸟经常飞来栖息在一户人家的窗台上，女主人开始拿出食物喂它。很快，女主人便爱上了这只鸟儿，可这场爱恋并不般配。小鸟每天飞到窗前，女主人便每天捧出食物。恋情结束之后，小白鸟一去不复返，可女主人连着几年日复一日地把面包屑放到窗台上，任风把它们吹走。"

7 月的时候，他常常带她去划船。最令她尴尬的是，自己只能由查尔斯抱上抱下，她称这个为"货物装卸"。然而，对查尔斯来说，那些时刻好

handlings," as she came to call it, seemed to be the highlight of the outings. In the boat she felt helpless, unable to move around, sitting in one spot. Also, she was unable to swim, should the boat turn over. Charles didn't observe her discomfort; she did note how much he enjoyed being in control. When he called for her one day in early August, she refused to.

They would, instead, she said, go for a walk in which she would move herself by the strength of her own arms and he would walk beside her.

"Why don't you just rest your arms and let me push you?"

"No."

"Your arms will get sore. I've been helping you do it for three months now."

"I wheeled myself for 12 years before you came along."

"But I don't like having to walk beside you while you push yourself!"

"Do you think I liked sitting helpless in your boat every weekend for the past two months?"

He never considered this and was shocked into silence. Finally he said quietly, "I never realized that, Amy. You're in a wheelchair all the time—I never thought you'd mind sitting in the boat. It's the same thing."

"It is not the same thing. In this chair, I can move by myself; I can go anywhere I need to go. That boat traps me so I can't do anything—I couldn't even save myself if something happened and I fell out."

"But I'm there. Don't you think I could save you or help you move or whatever it is you want?"

"Yes, but Charles—the point is I've spent 12 years learning to manage by myself. I even live in a city that's miles from my family so I'll have to be independent and do things for myself. Being placed in the boat takes all that

像就是他们户外活动最精彩的那个部分。在船上她感到很无助，没法四处活动，只能坐在一个地方。而且一旦船翻了，她也不会游泳。查尔斯完全没有注意到她的不安；而她却发现了他是那么喜欢控制别人。8 月初的一天，他邀请她去划船，她拒绝了。

她建议他们出去散步，这样她就可以凭自己的手臂力量推动轮椅，他就可以走在她的身边。

“你为什么不让自己的胳膊休息一下，让我来推你呢？”

“不用。”

“你的胳膊会酸的，三个月以来一直是我在推你的呀！”

“可在你出现之前，我推了自己 12 年。”

“可我不愿让你自己推轮椅，而我却只是个旁观者！”

“你以为过去两个月的每个周末，我就喜欢无可奈何地坐在你的船上吗？”

他一时间惊讶得说不出话，因为他从未考虑过这点。最后他平静地说道：“我从未意识到这一点，艾米。你一直坐在轮椅里——我没想过你会介意我让你坐在船上。我以为这是一码事。”

“这不是一回事。坐在轮椅上，我还能行动自如，想去哪里就能去哪里；而那条船却把我困住了，它让我感到无奈——万一发生了意外，我掉进了水里，我甚至都无法自救。”

“可是有我在啊！难道你觉得我救不了你，不能帮你活动或是干你任何想干的事吗？”

I've won away from me. Can't you see why I object to it? I don't want to feel helpless."

As they went down the path Charles selfishly only thought of his own needs, finally he lost control and said, "Amy, I need to have you dependent upon me." He grabbed the wheelchair and pushed her along. She had to let go of the wheels or injure herself. He could not see the anger in her eyes, and it was just as well for it was an anger he would not have understood.

She would not answer her telephone the next morning but in his mail that afternoon came an envelope that he knew had come from Amy. The handwriting was not beautiful, but it was without question hers. Inside was only a card on which she had written:

If you want something badly enough,

You must let it go free.

If it comes back to you,

It's yours.

If it doesn't,

You really never had it anyway.

(Anonymous)

He ran out of his apartment, refusing to believe that Amy might no longer be in her home. As he was running towards her apartment, he kept hearing a roar in his ears: "You must let it go free; you must let it go free."

But he thought: I can't risk it, she is mine, can't give her a chance not to belong to me, can't let her think she doesn't need me, she must need me. Oh God, I have to have her.

But her apartment was empty. Somehow in the hours overnight, she had

“你能。可是，查尔斯——关键是我花了12年的时间才学会自理。我甚至搬到离家几英里远的城市，就是为了让自己独立，一切都由自己动手。把我放在船上等于剥夺了我所获得的一切。难道你不明白我为什么反对你那样做吗？我不想让自己感到无助。”

他们沿着小路继续往前走着，自私的查尔斯只顾自己的需求，最后他失去了控制，说道：“艾米，我需要你依赖着我。”他一把抓过轮椅，推着她飞跑起来。无奈她只好放开轮子，免得伤了自己。他看不到她眼中的愤怒，这样也好，因为那种愤怒不是他所能理解的。

第二天清晨，她没有接他打来的电话。可下午的时候，查尔斯收到的信件中有一封信，他知道那一定是艾米写给自己的。字写得虽不漂亮，但可以肯定那就是她的笔迹。信封里只有一张卡片，上面写着：

如果你渴望爱情，
就必须给它自由。
倘若鸟儿回还，
它就不再飞走。
若它去无影踪，
你从未真正拥有。
（无名氏）

他冲出公寓，不肯相信艾米会搬家。他朝她的公寓狂奔而去，一路上只有一个声音在他耳边萦绕：“给它自由；你必须给它自由！”

可他心想：我不能冒这个险，她是我的，我决不允许她不再属于我，决不允许她有不再需要我的想法，她一定需要我。噢，上帝，我必须得到她！

然而她的公寓早已人去楼空。她一定是在头天夜里花了几个小时收拾

packed—by herself—and moved by herself. The rooms were now impersonal; their cold stillness could not respond when he fell to the floor and sobbed.

By the middle of August he had heard nothing from Amy. He went often to the park but avoided looking for the white bird.

September came and had almost gone before he finally received a letter. The handwriting was without question hers. The postmark was that of a city many miles distant. He tore open the envelope and at first thought it was empty. Then he noticed a single white feather had fallen from it. In his mind, the white bird rose in flight and its wings let fly one feather. Were it not for the feather, no one would have known that the white bird had ever been. Thus he knew Amy would not be back, and it was many hours before he let the feather drop out of his hand.

好行李——自己动手——然后离开的。此时此刻，房间里再也找不到任何生命的气息。他倒在地板上啜泣，回答他的只有一片阴冷的寂静。

到了 8 月中旬，他依然没收到艾米的任何消息。他还是常常上公园，但总是刻意地不愿看见那只白色的小鸟。

来也匆匆去也匆匆的 9 月，他终于收到了一封熟悉的来信，毫无疑问那就是她的笔迹。邮戳表明这封信来自另一个遥远的城市。他撕开信封，最初以为里面什么也没有，后来才发现那根从信封中飘落的洁白羽毛。他的脑海里浮现出那只小白鸟，它展翅高飞，一片羽毛从它的翅上飘落。若不是小白鸟离去时留下了这片羽毛，试问有谁会知道它曾经来过呢？于是，他终于明白：艾米再也不会回来了。好几个钟头之后，那根羽毛才从他的手中悄然滑落。

The Love Letter

迟到的情书

◎ Any Joystiq

I was always a little in awe of Great-aunt Stephina Roos. Indeed, as children we were all frankly terrified of her. The fact that she did not live with the family, preferring her tiny cottage and **solitude**① to the comfortable but rather noisy household where we were brought up—added to the respectful fear in which she was held.

We used to take it in turn to carry small **delicacies**② which my mother had made down from the big house to the little cottage where Aunt Stephia and an old colored maid spent their days. Old Tnate Sanna would open the door to the rather frightened little messenger and would usher him—or her—into the dark voor-kamer, where the shutters were always closed to keep out the heat and the flies. There we would wait, in trembling but not altogether unpleasant.

She was a tiny little woman to inspire so much veneration. She was always dressed in black, and her dark clothes melted into the shadows of the voor-kamer and made her look smaller than ever. But you felt the moment she entered that

---

① solitude ['sɔlitju:d] n. 孤独；隐居；荒凉（之地）

② delicacy ['delikəsi] n. 精美，娇嫩，优雅，敏感，微妙，棘手

美丽语录

Life has taught us that love does not consist in gazing at each other but in looking outward together in the same direction.

生活告诉我们，爱不在于朝夕相伴，而应能风雨同舟。

我对斯蒂菲娜老姑总是怀着些许敬畏之情。说实话，我们几个孩子都很怕她。她不和家人住在一起，宁愿住在她的小屋里，也不愿住在舒适、热闹的家里——我们都是在家里长大的——这更加重了我们对她的敬畏之情。

我们经常轮流从我们住的大房子里带些母亲亲手为她做的可口食物到那间小屋去，她和一名黑人女仆就住在那儿。桑娜老姨会为每一个上门的胆小的小使者开门，将他——或她——领进昏暗的客厅。那里的百叶窗总是关着的，以防热气和苍蝇跑进来。我们总是在那里颤抖着、但又不是完全不高兴地等待着斯蒂菲娜老姑。

虽然她身材纤细，但却赢得我们如此的尊敬。她总是穿着黑衣服，暗色的衣服和客厅里的暗影融为一体，把她的身材衬得更加娇小了。但她进

something vital and strong and somehow indestructible had come in with her, although she moved slowly, and her voice was sweet and soft.

She never embraced us. She would greet us and take out hot little hands in her own beautiful cool one, with blue veins standing out on the back of it, as though the white skin were almost too delicate to contain them.

Tante Sanna would bring in dishes of sweet, sweet, sticky candy, or a great bowl of grapes or peaches, and Great-aunt Stephina would converse gravely about happenings on the farm, and, more rarely, of the outer world.

When we had finished our sweetmeats or fruit she would accompany us to the stoep, bidding us thank our mother for her gift and sending **quaint**[①], old-fashioned messages to her and the Father. Then she would turn and enter the house, closing the door behind, so that it became once more a place of mystery.

As I grew older I found, rather to my surprise, that I had become genuinely fond of my aloof old great-aunt. But to this day I do not know what strange impulse made me take George to see her and to tell her, before I had confided in another living soul, of our engagement. To my astonishment, she was delighted.

"An Englishman," she exclaimed. "But that is splendid, splendid. And you," she turned to George, "you are making your home in this country? You do not intend to return to England just yet?"

She seemed relieved when she heard that George had bought a farm near our own farm and intended to settle in South Africa. She became quite animated, and chattered away to him.

After that I would often slip away to the little cottage by the mealie lands. Once she was somewhat disappointed on hearing that we had decided to wait for

① quaint [kweint] adj. 古雅的；奇特而有趣的；古怪的

门的那一刻，我们立即就能感到一种莫名的、充满活力和刚毅的气息，尽管她的步调缓慢、声音甜美轻柔。

她从来不会拥抱我们，但她会和我们寒暄，用她那双漂亮但却冷冰冰的手握住我们热乎乎的小手，她的手背上有一些青筋，好像手上白嫩的皮肤细薄得遮不住它们似的。

桑娜老姨每次都会端出几碟粘乎乎的糖果，或者一碗葡萄或是桃子给我们吃。斯蒂菲娜老姑则一本正经地说着那些发生在农场里的事，偶尔也谈些外面世界发生的事。

等我们吃完糖果或水果后，她会送我们到屋前的门廊，并且叮嘱我们要代她感谢母亲给她送食物，还要我们给父母带去一些奇怪的老式祝愿。接着她就转身回屋，随手关上门，让那里再次成为神秘世界。

我慢慢长大后惊奇地发现，我打心眼里开始喜欢我的那位孤伶伶的老姑了。至今我仍不知道是什么样的奇异动力让我在还没有告诉别人之前就把乔治领去看望老姑，并告诉她我们已经订婚的消息。让我感到意外的是，她听到这个消息后，竟非常高兴。

“是英国人！”她大声喊道，“太好了，真的太好了。你，”她转向乔治，“你要在这儿定居吗？你还不打算回国吧？”

当她听说乔治已经买下我们农场附近的一片农场并打算在南非定居下来时，她好像松了一口气，接着开始兴致勃勃地和乔治攀谈起来。

从此以后，我便成了玉米地边那间小屋的常客。有一次，当她听说我

two years before getting married, but when she learned that my father and mother were both pleased with the match she seemed reassured.

Still, she often appeared anxious about my love affair, and would ask questions that seemed to me strange, almost as though she feared that something would happen to destroy my romance. But I was quite unprepared for her outburst when I mentioned that George thought of paying a lightning visit to England before we were married."He must not do it," she cried."Ina, you must not let him go. Promise me you will prevent him." she was trembling all over. I did what I could to console her, but she looked so tired and pale that I persuaded her to go to her room and rest, promising to return the next day.

When I arrived I found her sitting on the stoep. She looked lonely and pathetic, and for the first time I wondered why no man had ever taken her and looked after her and loved her. Mother had told me that Great-aunt Stephina had been lovely as a young girl, and although no trace of that beauty remained, except perhaps in her brown eyes, yet she looked so small and appealing that any man, one felt, would have wanted to protect her.

She paused, as though she did not quite know how to begin.

Then she seemed to give herself, mentally, a little shake. "You must have wondered," she said, "Why I was so upset at the thought of young George's going to England without you. I am an old woman, and perhaps I have the silly fancies of the old, but I should like to tell you my own love story, and then you can decide whether it is wise for your man to leave you before you are married."

"I was quite a young girl when I first met Richard Weston. He was an Englishman who boarded with the Van Rensburgs on the next farm, four or five miles from us. Richard was not strong. He had a weak chest, and the doctors

们决定再过两年结婚时，脸上露出了失望的表情，但一听说我的父母都很满意这门亲事时，她就放心了。

但她还是经常把我的婚姻大事挂在嘴边，还常常问一些对我而言很奇怪的问题，就好像深怕我的婚事会告吹一样。当我提到乔治打算在结婚之前回国一趟时，她竟激动了起来，这完全出乎我的意料。只见她大声嚷道："他不能回去！爱娜！你不能放他走，你得答应我不放他走！"她整个人都在颤抖。我尽力安慰她，但她还是显得疲乏苍白。我只好劝她回屋休息，并答应第二天再来看她。

当我第二天去看她的时候，她正坐在屋前的门廊上。她看上去很孤单、很可怜。我第一次感到纳闷：以前怎么没有人娶她、照顾她和疼爱她呢？记得母亲曾经说过，斯蒂菲娜老姑曾是一个楚楚动人的年轻姑娘，尽管她的美貌早已消逝不见，除了那双褐色眼睛还残留些许昔日的风韵。不过她看上去还是那样娇小玲珑、惹人爱怜，让男人们忍不住想要保护她。

她欲言又止，好像不知该从何说起。

接着，她好像振作了起来，颤抖着说道："听你说乔治要回国，却又不带着你，我心里非常不安。你肯定很想知道原因吧！我是一个老太婆了，但我大概还怀着老人的那颗痴心。不过，我想把我的爱情故事讲给你听，这样你就能明白该不该在结婚之前让你的未婚夫离开你。"

"我第一次遇见理查德·威斯顿时还是一个很年轻的姑娘。他是英国人，寄宿在范·伦斯堡家里，离我家四、五英里远的一个农场上。他身体不好，

had sent him to South Africa so that the dry air could cure him. He taught the Van Rensburg children, who were younger than I was, though we often played together, but he did this for pleasure and not because he needed money.

"We loved one another from the first moment we met, though we did not speak of our love until the evening of my eighteenth birthday. All our friends and relatives had come to my party, and in the evening we danced on the big old carpet which we had laid down in the barn. Richard had come with the Van Rensburgs, and we danced together as often as we dared, which was not very often, for my father hated the Uitlanders. Indeed, for a time he had quarreled with Mynheer Van Rensburg for allowing Richard to board with him, but afterwards he got used to the idea, and was always polite to the Englishman, though he never liked him.

"That was the happiest birthday of my life, for while we were resting between dances Richard took me outside into the cool, moonlit night, and there, under the stars, he told me he loved me and asked me to marry him. Of course I promised I would, for I was too happy to think of what my parents would say, or indeed of anything except Richard was not at our meeting place as he had arranged. I was disappointed but not alarmed, for so many things could happen to either of us to prevent out keeping our tryst. I thought that next time we visited the Van Ransburgs, I should hear what had kept him and we could plan further meetings...

"So when my father asked if I would drive with him to Driefontein I was delighted. But when we reached the homestead and were sitting on the stoep drinking our coffee, we heard that Richard had left quite suddenly and had gone back to England. His father had died, and now he was the heir and must go back

胸闷气短。医生让他去南非，利用干燥的气候来治病。他给伦斯堡的孩子们上课，那些孩子的年纪都 比我小。尽管我们经常玩在一块，但理查德是以教书为乐，而不是为了赚钱。”

“我和理查德是一见钟情，尽管直到我 18 岁生日那晚我们才表示彼此的爱慕之情。那天我们所有亲友都来参加我的生日舞会。那晚，理查德也同伦斯堡先生来了，我们就在仓房里铺上一条宽大的旧毛毯，翩翩起舞。我和他鼓起勇气一齐跳了好多次，可其实也没多少次，因为我父亲很讨厌外国人。有一次，他还抱怨说伦斯堡先生不应该让理查德住在他家里，为此还吵了一架，不过他后来也习惯了。虽说一直不喜欢，但他对这个英国人还是以礼相待。

“那是我一生中最快乐的一个生日，因为在跳舞间歇时，理查德把我带到室外，沐浴着清凉的月光，在点点繁星之下，他对我倾诉爱慕之情，并向我求婚。我二话没说就答应了他的请求，因为我早已心花怒放，甚至来不及考虑父母会说些什么。一次约会，理查德没有出现在约定地点。我很失落，但却没有觉得奇怪，因为我们的约会经常会被许多事情耽搁。我想下一次我们拜访伦斯堡家时，我就能知道他失约的原因，这样我们就能安排接下来的约会了……

“所以当我的父亲叫我开车送他去德里方丹时，我高兴极了。可当我们到达伦斯堡家的农场，坐在他们屋前的门廊上喝咖啡时，却听说理查德已经不辞而别回英国去了。他的父亲去世了，他是继承人，所以必须回国处

to look after his estates.

"I do not remember very much more about that day, except that the sun seemed to have stopped shining and the country no longer looked beautiful and full of promise, but bleak and desolate as it sometimes does in winter or in times of drought. Late that afternoon, Jantje, the little Hottentot herd boy, came up to me and handed me a letter, which he said the English baas had left for me. It was the only love letter I ever received, but it turned all my bitterness and grief into a peacefulness which was the nearest I could get, then, to happiness. I knew Richard still loved me, and somehow, as long as I had his letter, I felt that we could never be really parted, even if he were in England and I had to remain on the farm. I have it yet, and though I am an old, tired woman, it still gives me hope and courage."

"I must have been a wonderful letter, Aunt Stephia," I said.

The old lady came back from her dreams of that far-off romance. "Perhaps," she said, hesitating a little, "perhaps, my dear, you would care to read it?"

"I should love to, Aunt Stephia," I said gently.

She rose at once and tripped into the house as eagerly as a young girl. When she came back she handed me a letter, faded and yellow with age, the edges of the envelope worn and frayed as though it had been much handled. But when I came to open it I found that the seal was unbroken.

"Open it, open it," said Great-aunt Stephia, and her voice was shaking.

I broke the seal and read.

It was not a love letter in the true sense of the word, but pages of the minutest directions of how "my sweetest Phina" was to elude her father's vigilance, creep down to the drift at night and there meet Jantje with a horse

理那些遗产。

“我已经记不清那天的情形了，只是记得那天的阳光显得暗淡，田野也不再美丽和充满海誓山盟，萧瑟凄凉得如同冬日或大旱时期。那天下午晚些时候，霍但托特族的小牧童詹杰交给我一封信，他说是那位英国先生留给我的。这是我收到的唯一一封情书，可它把我的忧伤一扫而光，让我的心平静下来，可以说是一种类似幸福的平静。我知道理查德还爱着我，不知道为什么，自从我收到他的信之后，我觉得我们不会真正分手，即使他身在英国而我却只能呆在这里。这封信我保留至今，虽然我已是一个年老体衰的老太婆，但它仍旧能给我带来勇气和希望。”

“斯蒂菲娜老姑，那封信一定很美吧！”我说。

老太太从她那久远的爱之梦中醒过神来。“也许，”她带着忧郁说道，"也许，亲爱的，你想看看那封信吧？"

“我很想看，斯蒂菲娜老姑。”我轻声说道。

她猛地一下站起来，奔进屋里，急切得像个年轻姑娘。她从屋里出来后，递给我一封信。岁月已让那封信褪色发黄，信封边也已经磨损，看上去好像被摩挲过无数次。但在启信时，我发现封口还没有拆开。

“打开它，打开它。”斯蒂菲娜老姑说道，她的声音在颤抖。

我撕开封口，开始念信。

严格说来，它算不上是一封情书，而只是几页内容详尽的行动指南。信中交代了“我最亲爱的菲娜”该如何摆脱她父亲的监视，在夜间时分逃出家门，詹杰会在浅滩上牵马等着她，然后将她驮到史密斯多普，到了那

which would take her to Smitsdorp. There she was to go to "my true friend, Henry Wilson", who would give her money and make arrangements for her to follow her lover to Cape Town and from there to England," where, my love, we can be married at once. But if, my dearest, you are not sure that you can face lift with me in a land strange to you, then do not take this important step, for I love you too much to wish you the smallest unhappiness. If you do not come, and if I do not hear from you, then I shall know that you could never be happy so far from the people and the country which you love. If, however, you feel you can keep your promise to me, but are of too timid and modest a journey to England unaccompanied, then write to me, and I will, by some means, return to fetch my bride."

I read no further.

"But Aunt Phina!" I gasped. "Why... why...?"

The old lady was watching me with trembling eagerness, her face flushed and her eyes bright with expectation. "Read it aloud, my dear," she said. "I want to hear every word of it. There was never anyone I could trust... Uitlanders were hated in my young days... I could not ask anyone."

"But, Auntie, don't you even know what he wrote?"

The old lady looked down, troubled and shy like a child who has unwittingly done wrong.

"No, dear," she said, speaking very low. "You see, I never learned to read."

里再去找理查德的“知心朋友亨利·威尔逊”，他会给她钱为她作好安排，使她能跟随她的情人到开普敦，随后转道英国。“亲爱的，这样我们就可以在英国结婚了。但是我的至爱，如果你不能保证你能在一个陌生的地方和我一块生活，你就不必采取这个重大行动，因为我太爱你了，不能让你感到丝毫不快。如果你不来，如果我听不到你的回音，我就会知道，如果你离开你挚爱的亲人和乡土，你是不会幸福的。但如果你能实践你对我的承诺，而由于你生性持重胆怯不愿单身前往英国，就来信告诉我，那我就会想方设法回南非来迎接我的新娘。”

我没有继续念下去。

“可是，菲娜老姑！”我气喘吁吁地问道：“为什么……为什么……？”

老太太的身体颤抖着，她渴望知道信的内容，她的双眼炯炯有神地凝视着我，急切的期待让她脸颊泛红。“亲爱的，大声念吧！”她说，“信里的每句话，我都要听！当时我找不到可靠的人给我念……在我年轻时，外国人是被人深恶痛绝的……我找不到人给我念啊！”

“可是老姑，难道你一直不知道信的内容吗？”

老太太低下了头，像一个无心犯了错的孩子那样怯生生的，不知道该说些什么。

“不知道，亲爱的，”她低声说道，“你也知道，我从来没有念过书啊！”

Why We Fall Out of Love
为什么我们不爱了

◎ Laura Schaefer

Very often, we find that two people who come together out of love grow apart as the years go by. Why does this happen?

Let's say you planted a coconut tree and a mango tree in your garden when they were young saplings, and they were the same height. You thought they would get along pretty well, a great love affair! And if both of them remained stunted and never grew, they would remain compatible. But if both of them grow to their full potential, they will grow to different heights, shapes and possibilities.

If you are looking for sameness between two people, the relationship will always fall apart. After all, a man and a woman come together because they are different. So it is the differences that brought you together, and the differences may become starker and more manifest as one grows. Unless you learn to enjoy the differences as you grow, falling apart or growing apart will naturally happen. If you are expecting both people to grow in the same direction and in the same way, that is unfair to both people. It will curtail and suffocate both of their lives. Whether you fall apart in years, in months or in days simply depends on how fast you are growing.

美丽语录

Before finding the right people, the only need to do is to make yourself good enough.

在找到合适的人之前，唯一需要做的，就是让自己足够的优秀。

我们身边经常会看到这样的一对：他们因为爱情走到了一起，却在多年后分开了。这样的事儿为什么会发生?

我来打个比方吧：你在花园里种了一棵椰子树和一棵芒果树的小树苗，它们栽下去的时候高度相同。你以为它们会相处得很好，多好的一对啊！是的，如果它们都发育不良，长不高，它们彼此会相处得很好。但如果它们都发挥了充分的潜能生长着，那它们会长成不同的高度和形状，就有了许多的可能性。

如果你总在寻找两人之间的共同之处，那么这段关系多半会无疾而终。男人和女人之所以走到一起，正是因为彼此间的不同。正是这些差异吸引着对方走到一起，而随着每个人的成长，这些差异也会越发明显。如果你无法在彼此成长的过程中享受这种越来越大的差异，那么你们自然就会出现隔阂，甚至分手。如果你期望双方都能朝着同一个方向用同样的方式成长，这对谁来说都是不公平的，这也会令对方压抑窒息，剥夺彼此的生活乐趣。所以分开只是时间问题，你们的爱情是有几年、几个月还是几天的生命，仅仅取决于你们的成长速度。

This whole expectation that the person who partners with you should be just like you is a sure way to destroy a relationship. It is a sure way to destroy the garden. Allow, nurture and enjoy the differences between you and your partner. Otherwise, the situation will be maintained in such a way where one person is compulsively dependent upon the other, or both people are compulsively dependent upon each other.

We need to understand that relationships happen because of certain needs—physical, emotional and psychological needs. Whatever the nature of the relationship, the fundamental aspect is you have a need to be fulfilled. We may claim many things for why we have formed a relationship, but if those needs and expectations are not fulfilled, relationships will go bad.

And as people grow and mature, these needs change. When these needs change, what looked like everything between two people will not feel the same after some time. But we do not have to base a relationship on these same needs forever and feel that the relationship is over. We can always make the relationship mature into something else.

Whatever the needs that brought people together need not be the fundamentals of a relationship forever. The very fundamentals of a relationship have to change as time passes, and as one ages and matures in many different ways. If that change is not made, growing apart or falling apart is definitely a certainty.

期待自己的伴侣同自己一样，这必然只会毁掉一段感情，就像期待椰子树和芒果树一样长大会毁了你的花园一样。允许你们之间存在不同，培养并享受这种差异性。否则你们的关系就会维持这样一种状态：其中一方被迫依赖于另一方，或者双方都被迫性地依赖彼此。

我们需要明白，一段感情是因为某些需求才会产生：生理需求、情感需求和心理需求。不论感情的性质是什么，一段感情最基础的部分就是你有一个需求需要满足。我们可能会对一段感情要求很多，可是当这些需求和期望无法实现的时候，感情就会变质。

随着人们的长大和成熟，这些需求也会发生变化。而当需求变化时，两个人之间的一切似乎也都随着时间发生了变化。我们不要认为那些永恒不变的需求才是感情的基础，不要觉得需求变化了感情也就结束了。我们的关系其实可以更成熟。

虽然是各种需求让两个人走到一起，但是想要关系长久稳定，这些需求并不是根本。随着时间的推移、年龄的增长以及各方面的逐渐成熟，感情的根本也会发生变化。如果没有变化，那么感情的结局必然只会是隔阂和分开。

I've learned...

That love, not time, heals all wounds.

我懂了……

治愈一切创伤的并非是时间，而是爱啊。